Getting to the
Root

Confronting Issues of the Heart

KEITH BOUDREAUX

Legacy Press

Getting to the Root

Published by: Legacy Press
P.O. Box 773096
Houston, Texas 77215-3096
(281) 531-5014

Cover and illustrations
by alpha & omega DESIGN
Website: alphaomegadesign.com

ISBN: 0-7392-0346-0

Printed in the USA by

MORRIS PUBLISHING

3212 East Highway 30 • Kearney, NE 68847 • 1-800-650-7888

To my beloved Celeste:
your vision inspires my faith,
your encouragement gives me hope,
and your self-sacrifice teaches me love.

CONTENTS

Introduction   1

1. *ANGER*
   A. A Woman Called Mara   15
   B. The Grim Garygoyle of Anger   19

2. *ENVY*
   A. A Witch and a King   29
   B. The Black Raven of Envy   32

3. *PRIDE*
   A. The Prophet Bigot   43
   B. The Siberian Winter of Pride   45

4. *SLOTH*
   A. The Disillusioned King   57
   B. The Relentless Termites of Sloth   61

5. *GLUTTONY*
   A. He Died a Slave   73
   B. The Seductive Sirens of Gluttony   76

6. *GREED*
   A. The Miser Becomes a Traitor   87
   B. The Glittering Mirage of Greed   90

7. *LUST*
   A. How the Mighty Have Fallen   101
   B. The Kryptonite of Lust   104

Conclusion: The Final Healing   115

Notes   130

NOTE TO THE READER

In this book you will find seven stories from the Bible which have been adapted, embellished and shaped to suit a specific purpose. In every case, care was taken to remain faithful to the Scriptural intent of each one. Take them for what they are: illustrations to shed light upon Biblical truths. The eighth and last story, "The Final Healing," is a purely fictional account of life in the hereafter. Its purpose is to stimulate and challenge your thinking, not so much about heaven, but rather about the every day realities of sacrifice, evil, love and shame.

Secondly, this book should not be read as a "how-to" manual to overcome sin. Instead, it is more of a "how-God" handbook, for it is he who defeats sin in our lives through three of his most blessed gifts: faith, hope and love.

Finally, I wish to acknowledge and thank my informal "reading committee" for their input and encouragement: my mother, Bobbie Boudreaux; my sister, Kathy Welch; Rev. Van Lees; Rev. Don Jonker and Rev. David Kent. Very special thanks to my wife, Celeste, for her many hours of editing and typesetting and for her refusal to accept anything less than the best.

INTRODUCTION

More than twenty years ago, a Scottish friend told me the most amazing story. He was on a missionary trip with two single women to Eastern Europe. Every evening, the women would sleep in a pup tent and he slept in the van, which had a built-in stove and sink. One day, he woke up, bleary-eyed, and reached for the kettle to heat up water for tea. In his early morning confusion, he made a mistake. Instead of putting the kettle on the stove, he picked up a container of gasoline! It didn't take long for an explosion to occur, hurling him out of the van like a cannonball. He stood there in his underwear and watched helplessly while the entire vehicle burned up, along with his clothes and personal effects. After the fire was out, he did manage to find his half-burned passport, which he had to present to his embassy for replacement in order to leave the country. As he told the story, he had a good sense of humor about it, and we all shared a laugh together.

It occurred to me that this is an excellent picture of the nature of sin. The Greek word for sin, *hamartia*, means "a missing of the mark," a mistake. It is a reaching for the wrong substance, done sometimes in ignorance and sometimes deliberately, yet always with serious consequences. Like my Scottish friend, who was forced to walk through downtown Bucharest in his underwear, sin creates a deep sense of shame and embarrassment which only compounds the problem more.

We are in a fight for our very lives, the importance of which could not be more serious. On my bookshelf at home sits a fascinating volume titled The Fifteen Decisive Battles of the World by the nineteenth century British historian, Sir Edward Creasy.[1] Beginning with the battle of Marathon in 490 BC and ending with Waterloo in 1815, Creasy highlights the importance of each conflict and poses the same question: "What would have happened if the 'other side' had won?" For example, in 732 AD, the seemingly irresistible force of the Muslim advance clashed with Christian Europe at the Battle of Tours. Charles Martel, by

1

preventing their invasion of ancient France, preserved Christendom from a hostile takeover. Many historians have noted that were it not for the victory of the Europeans at Tours, the Koran would today be the most cherished book in the West, rather than the Bible. Great battles, indeed, have great consequences.

> # We have landed behind enemy lines. In addition to being outnumbered and outgunned, we discover a traitor in the camp.

If I were to change Creasy's title to <u>The Single Most Decisive Battle of the World</u>, it would not be a description of a military struggle, but rather a spiritual one. For the truth is that the most important, most decisive war in history is the one that is waged in the human heart between good and evil. This battle is actually a conflict -- a civil war, if you will -- between what we have been (sinners) and what we are becoming (saints).

The bad news is that we have landed behind enemy lines. We find ourselves in a hostile environment that continually tempts us in the wrong direction. However, that's not the worst of it, for in addition to being outnumbered and outgunned, we discover a traitor in the camp. Actually, not just one but seven: pride, envy, anger, sloth, gluttony, greed and lust. These are our worst enemies who continually sabotage our best efforts to defeat the occupying forces of evil.

Happily, there does exist an underground resistance movement led by faith, hope and love. They are our allies. They empower us to win many victories and come running with the stretchers when we lie wounded on the battlefield. No risk is too great for them and no soldier too hopeless. Their victory is assured by the liberating forces stationed just outside our field of view. The battle lines have been drawn. The importance of the outcome is incalculable. It is by far the most decisive battle in the world.

THE SEVEN DEADLY SINS

The seven deadly sins appeared early in Christian history with the famous monastic leader John Cassian (d.433 AD) and also Gregory the Great (540-604 AD), who eventually became pope.[2] However, long before the church came into existence, many Jewish thinkers and rabbis dealt with great insight into a number of these sins. Not only that, but such notable Greek philosophers as Aristotle, Seneca and Plutarch analyzed their pathology and proposed solutions which still strike today's reader as very sensible and helpful. Thus, whether one is a pagan, a Jew, or a Christian, or whether one lived during classical, medieval or modern times, these sins are still just as relevant and just as deadly as they ever were.

Family	Member Sins		
1. PRIDE	*Anger*	*Envy*	*Pride*
2. SLOTH	*Sloth*		
3. LUST	*Gluttony*	*Greed*	*Lust*

In this book, I have divided the seven sins into the three categories or "family clusters" of pride, sloth and lust.

A. The PRIDE Family: Anger, Envy & Pride

Anger and envy belong with pride, for they all three share striking similarities. The most common reasons we become angry are because we have been stopped from getting our own way, have been insulted by someone else, or have had our rights violated. Each of these cases provoke our anger by reminding us that we are not all-powerful or all-knowing. What is frustration, if not the chafing of our imagination and creativity

3

against the prison house of time, place and mortality? Pride does not like to be reminded of its limitations.

Envy is surely an outgrowth of pride. The awards and successes of others cause such pain to an envious person precisely because he thinks too highly of himself. Only a humble man can genuinely rejoice in the greater accomplishments of his friends or family. He can admire people, which is a delicious pleasure denied to the envious.

B. The LUST Family: Gluttony, Greed & Lust

Gluttony and greed are obviously near cousins to the deeper sin of lust. One could even say that they are different forms of lust. All three take what are basically good, essential elements of life and pervert them through excess. Lust does it with sex, greed with money, and gluttony with food or drink. The sins of appetite on this side of the aisle clearly proceed from an ungrateful heart.

Imagine for a moment that on your son's graduation from high school, you present him with a beautiful, brand new, red Ferrari. (Forget about the wisdom of that for a moment!) As you hand him the keys, you say, "Enjoy this car. Your mother and I give it to you simply because we love you." He throws his arms around you both, hops in the Ferrari and takes off a little faster than you would like! A few weeks go by and you notice the car is not as shiny as it used to be. There is a bit of mud on the front bumper and when you open the door, sand from the beach spills out. You mention this to your son and he absent-mindedly says, "Don't worry, I'll clean it up." But he doesn't. More time passes and the Ferrari is looking worse and worse. Finally, one day a wrecker pulls up to your home dragging -- you guessed it -- the once highly tuned, world class car. It seems that your son forgot to put the screw back in when he changed the oil. The engine is ruined and the car undrivable.

This is precisely the nature of gluttony, greed and lust. Each one takes a wonderful gift from God and through ungratefulness misuses and eventually ruins it. These sins turn the blessings of food, money and sex into destructive,

4

dysfunctional forces that eventually bring us nothing but sorrow and shame.

C. SLOTH:

Sloth is in a category all by itself. It is at least as ruinous as pride or lust. Many of us cry out to God when trouble comes our way. We are energized and focused as we fight the crocodiles and hunt for the land mines before they explode. Yet, when things improve and life gets a bit softer, sloth begins to whisper in our ears, immobilizing our resolve and suffocating our spirits. The fixed stare and glassy eyes of sloth can be one of the most difficult of sins to overcome.

GETTING TO THE ROOT

A word of explanation is in order concerning the tree and root system used as the primary symbol in this book. People often think of sin as crimes such as murder or theft, or bad behavior such as lying or cheating on one's spouse. These outward actions are certainly sin, but, like the branches of a tree, they are only part of the plant. The origin of sin lies deep beneath the surface, like the root system of a tree. Most outward sins can be traced back to one or more of the seven "root" sins.

The job of parents, teachers, and law enforcement is to prune back the outward fruits of sin by regulating behavior. However, these social institutions have no real power to change the underlying roots. Thus, while a person may be restrained from committing murder (snip the branch), he is still guilty of the root sin of anger. His anger will continue to cause "sprouts" of various kinds of negative behavior: quarreling, violent or abusive outbursts, cursing, and so on. However, if the root of anger is removed -- or, rather, transformed into the virtue of forgiveness -- then even the *temptation* towards not only murder, but all these other related sins, is eliminated.

The old roots must die and be replaced by a new system, based on the nature of Jesus Christ. Who is able to accomplish this? Not society, not the church, not even we, ourselves! Only

5

the power of God is able to transform the evil roots of sin in our hearts into his likeness.

THEOLOGICAL VIRTUES

Thomas Aquinas, the great Medieval theologian, made a distinction between what he called the "Cardinal Virtues" of temperance, fortitude, justice and prudence and the "Theological Virtues" of faith, hope and love. While the former are necessary to live a moral life, they are inadequate by themselves. Rather, says Aquinas, faith, hope and love ". . . are called theological virtues: first, because their object is God, inasmuch as they direct us aright to God: secondly, *because they are infused in us by God alone*: thirdly, because these virtues are not made known to us, save by Divine revelation, contained in Holy Writ."[3] (emphasis mine) In other words, we cannot win the moral battle alone. There must be supernatural help, Divine infusion -- grace, from an outside source.

Theological Virtue	Blessing to the Believer	Specific Method of Combating Sin
FAITH	IDENTITY	Security in knowing who we are and where we fit in God's overall plan
HOPE	ENDURANCE	Rejuvenation, motivation and energy to keep us moving forward
LOVE	UNION	Satisfaction and contentment, which protect us from temptation

This is the difference between legalistic religion and a genuine relationship with Jesus Christ. Prudence, for example, may stop a woman from stealing a watch, but faith, hope and love can quench the greed that motivates her. Fortitude may cause a man to get out of bed every morning and go to a job that he hates, but hope can discover meaning and purpose in the most mundane of situations. Hope can also inspire him to pursue a more fulfilling course of action.

The point is that we overcome sin in the same way that we come to know God: by grace alone. Without the supernatural power of faith, hope and love, we are doomed before we start. For, just as sin grows in us naturally, so does virtue. Each of us at birth received a bad seed from our father Adam which manifests itself in pride, anger, envy, sloth, gluttony, greed and lust (to name just a few!) The solution is to have a new seed planted by the Lord Jesus that produces faith, hope and love (to name just a few!) The old nature must die so that the new may thrive.

FAITH AND IDENTITY

"Tradition!" exclaims Tevye in the musical, *"Fiddler On The Roof."* Describing his Jewish heritage, he explains, "Because of our traditions, every one of us knows who he is and what God expects him to do."

It is not for nothing that throughout history, religious faith has inspired the most enduring and meaningful traditions in cultures all around the world. For it is our beliefs about God and ultimate reality that touch us in the deepest core of our being. Faith tells us where we fit in the grand scope of things and it blesses us with a rock solid sense of identity that nothing can destroy.

True faith creates a Copernican revolution within each individual. Just as the Polish astronomer, Copernicus, proved to the world that the earth revolved around the sun, so faith unequivocally demonstrates to us that our lives revolve around God. He is the center of the universe, not we.

Such knowledge both humbles and exalts in the proper way and at the proper times. While we understand and accept our small role in this vast universe, we also realize that we are blessed with a relationship to the one who created it all! In the Book of Revelation we are told that God will give each of us "a white stone with a new name written on it, known only to him who receives it." He knows us by name; what a wonder!

The loss of such identity, is, perhaps, the greatest tragedy secularism has bequeathed to modern man. It is certainly the culprit behind much of our dysfunctional society, from teenage suicide to escapism in drugs and entertainment. We wander from one pleasure to the next, blocking out the silences of God with the din of modern life. Like homeless princes who have forgotten their true heritage, we scavenge among the debris, hoping for some morsel of meaning. From time to time, distant memories fleetingly insinuate themselves into our consciousness. Memories of the king's palace and yearnings of nobility and dignity and self-sacrifice -- great deeds and heroic sentiments. Yet, they seem to evaporate as quickly as they appeared, leaving us shuffling along in a existential soup line.

Faith seeks us out. It lovingly calls us by name in the presence of our homeless compatriots and places a crown on our heads. Our dignity is restored as we kneel and sense the sword touching, first the right shoulder and then the left. We rise with the title of "sir" or "dame," our eyes clear and bright. At the same time, the earth shakes, the thunder rolls, and the presence of one far greater than ourselves begins to make his appearance. His glory is so overwhelming that we find ourselves prostrate before him, absent-mindedly casting our crowns at his feet.

Dignity and humility, identity and purpose are the great gifts bestowed on us by faith. Not only do these qualities strengthen us against sin, they also enable us to endure sin. For the longer I live as a Christian, the more profoundly I understand the depths of my own depravity. This also is the gift of identity: to realize that we are sinners. To admit freely and daily that we have sinned in thought, word and deed is not an admission of defeat but of glorious victory. We know who we are, we know where we have come from, and we understand the price that was paid for our redemption. Faith is an especially strong antidote to the self-centeredness of anger, the insecurity of envy and the conceit of pride.

HOPE AND ENDURANCE

Faith is rooted in history. From the covenant with Abraham to the giving of the law to the death and resurrection of Jesus Christ, faith always looks to the past. It is securely based on the historic inbreaking of God's kingdom on earth.

Hope, however, is just as firmly rooted in the future. Nowhere is this more true than in the belief of the Second Coming of Jesus Christ, which Paul calls the "blessed hope" in Titus 2:13. It is a hope that has been so deeply planted in every Christian heart that all churches from Catholic to Orthodox to Protestant list it as an article of faith. It is one of the non-negotiables of being a believer. We may disagree about whether or not a priest should marry or the fine points of church government, but there is no question when it comes to the Second Advent. I find this remarkable, because it is an event that still lies in the future. Moreover, for 2000 years, fanatics and charlatans have appeared who attempted to hijack this belief for their own purposes. By now, one would expect cynicism and ridicule at the very mention of the Second Coming, yet I find few Christians who are so inclined. Instead, as the Gospel continues to spread around the world at an unbelievable rate, more and more each day are having this hope planted in them. Rather than dying out, it continues to grow stronger, giving those who believe incredible courage and an eager expectation for the future.

> Faith is the cup, the container, that brings the cool waters of hope to a thirsty soul.

This is the rejuvenating power of hope which I like to call the "antioxidant" of the soul. Though our bodies age, our souls are being renewed day by day.[4]

This renewal of life and energy which attends hope is the reason why the Bible always associates it with endurance. Whereas faith saves us initially, hope is what keeps us saved, keeps us believing, keeps us trusting. For just as our faith is firmly rooted in Christ's finished work on the cross, so is our hope securely tied to Christ's finished work in us. Every time we fail and lay bloodied and defeated on the road, the Good Samaritan of hope picks us up and bandages our wounds. It refuses to give up.

Faith is the cup, the container, the structure that brings the cool waters of hope to a thirsty soul. It is an especially effective antidote to sloth, the growing indifference and apathy often associated with middle and old age. Hope keeps us young at heart.

LOVE AND UNION

Sin complicates while virtue simplifies. Sin corrodes while virtue purifies. Sin fragments while virtue unifies. If faith is rooted in the past and hope in the future, love is found in the present.[5] Love is the greatest and mightiest of all, for not only does it cover a multitude of sins, it also restores and heals the sinner as nothing else can.

From the songs I hear on the radio, I think our society would agree. From country and western to rock, from jazz to gospel to blues (especially blues), it seems that everyone is looking for love in all the wrong places. Like my Scottish friend mistakenly grabbing the can of gasoline, they are reaching out for one thing and ending up with something else altogether. This is especially true of those caught in the sins of gluttony, greed and lust. In all three, people are desperately trying to fill a void in their lives that was intended only for love.

The glutton attempts to fill that emptiness with food, drink or drugs; the greedy with money; and the lustful with sex. Their insatiable yearning is a desire for union with someone or something else.

The problem is that true love and true union are only accomplished by surrender and abandonment rather than sinful grasping. This is the great paradox behind the words of Jesus when he says; "For whoever wants to save his life will lose it, but whoever loses his life for me will find it."[6] True love will inevitably and necessarily produce self-denial and self-sacrifice, just as surely as lust produces selfishness. In order to love, we must give the priority to another.

10

Love deals sin a lethal blow by filling the empty spaces of the soul which breed the dark desires of evil. An overflowing heart of love acts as a secure guide, leading the hand past the deadly gasoline directly to the kettle of water waiting for morning tea.

Part One

ANGER

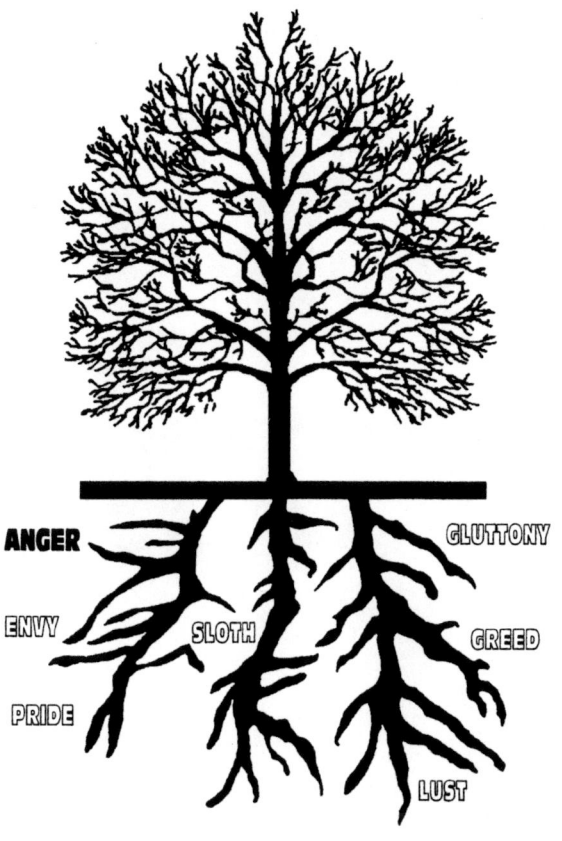

ANGER: Response to the thwarting of our wills, the violation of our rights or the narrowing of our options.

THE PERSPECTIVE OF FAITH: Gives us God's point of view, reminding us that we are not the center of the universe.

A WOMAN CALLED MARA

Elim bent down gingerly in what had become a ritual of sorts over the past few days. He watched as the dry, red dirt spilled from his hand onto the ground. Drought, famine, pestilence. These things were not supposed to happen to the people of God.

It had been a test. Should he leave Israel for greener pastures elsewhere, or stay and tough it out? That question had haunted him for weeks. His wife, Naomi, was dead set against leaving. Stubbornly, she refused any mention of moving. He had prayed that if God wanted them to stay, he would cause the dew to return, just as he had done for Gideon, yet nothing happened. The ground was as dry and lifeless as ever. "We will starve if we stay here," he thought.

Reluctantly, he turned to face his house. The hardest part would be convincing Naomi that this was the right thing to do. Then a thought occurred to him. Didn't Abraham, our great ancestor, go down to Egypt during times of famine? Not to mention Isaac and Jacob -- they did the same thing. A plan began to form in his mind. "Yes, we will leave for Moab tomorrow." The words shocked him as he said them out loud.

That evening was not a pleasant one in the household of Elimelech. In spite of his arguments and best logic, Naomi refused to budge. She seemed afraid that God would curse them if they left the Promised Land. She begged her husband not to take them to a foreign country -- especially Moab.

"Why, they practice human sacrifice there, Elim! It's a horrible, evil place."

"Wasn't Egypt a 'horrible, evil place,' as well, when Abraham went there for refuge? Naomi, we have no choice. We simply cannot afford to take the precious little seed we have left and waste it again on this useless piece of land."

"What about our sons?" she replied. "In just a few years they will be ready for marriage. Do you want them marrying Moabite women? That would be a sacrilege!"

"Naomi, I understand your fears. I share them myself. But what else can we do? At least in Moab there is a chance we can survive."

That night the family made a decision. Like hundreds of generations of families throughout history -- like Abraham -- they decided to search for better land. The consequences would be tragic. Much to her chagrin, both of Naomi's sons did indeed marry Moabite women: Orpah and Ruth. If that were not bad enough, though there was plenty of food to eat, Elim became sick. He could no longer work the ground. Naomi could not bear to watch her once robust and virile husband gradually grow more frail and decrepit. Thankfully, the two boys were able to take over, and for several years she devoted all of her time and energy to nursing her feeble husband.

"Oh Elim! How can I go on without you?"

She felt an anger rising up within her. She wanted to scream at him, "Didn't I tell you this would happen!" Yet when she looked at his emaciated body, the words evaporated.

Elim died, and ten years later, both of her sons began showing the same symptoms as their father. First, the coughing, then the long, slow, now familiar descent into the land of shadows. Now Naomi was thrice bereaved.

Then, as if to mock her even more, word came from Israel that the land was productive again. Food was plentiful and the famine only a dim memory. Naomi decided to return home.

Only one problem remained: what to do with her two daughters-in-law. Even though they were Moabites, she had developed a fondness for them, especially Ruth. During the difficult days of illness, Ruth had courageously tended to her husband and even successfully grew a small vegetable garden which kept food on the table.

"But now," Naomi thought, "what good are they to me or I to them? They belong here in Moab, not Israel." She fought the anger again that seemed to rear its head more frequently these days. "Completely alone! I left with a husband and two sons, now I return home with nothing."

Then the thought surfaced again. She had tried over and over to push it away, yet here it was insinuating itself, almost as if it had a life of its own. "God is to blame for this," it whispered. "He could have saved Elim; he could have saved the two boys -- but he didn't. He enjoys watching you suffer."

"He's probably laughing at me now," she thought. "What a sight we must be, three women returning to the land of 'promise.'" She spat the word out of her mouth. "What kind of promise is this? A promise of death, a promise of poverty, of starvation?"

The decision was made; she must return alone. The next morning she talked with Orpah and Ruth. "I must return to Israel, but you belong here in Moab. Please don't try to dissuade me; my mind is made up. I've been cursed by God, and if you stay with me, you will probably die also. Please, go home."

The three women dissolved into tears and sobs. They had been together such a long time and the hardships had only served to deepen the bonds between them. Reluctantly, Orpah agreed. There was no future for her in Israel. Naomi would be better off without her.

"God be with you," she said sadly, as she slowly turned and headed back toward town.

Ruth fell on her knees. She begged, "Please don't urge me to leave you or to turn back from you. Where you go I will go, and where you stay I will stay. Your people will be my people and your God my God. Where you die I will die, and there I will be buried. May the Lord deal with me, be it ever so severely, if anything but death separates you and me."

When Naomi saw the determined look in Ruth's eyes, she reluctantly agreed. They turned their faces west toward Israel and began the long journey home. When they arrived in Bethlehem, news quickly spread that Naomi and a stranger had arrived in town. After more than ten years and what seemed a thousand lifetimes, the women asked, "Can this be Naomi?"

"Don't call me Naomi any longer," she replied. "Call me Mara, because God has made my life very bitter. I went away full, but the Lord has brought me back empty. No more will I be known as Naomi, for God has become my enemy."

THE GRIM GARGOYLE OF ANGER

High atop a Gothic cathedral perches a twisted figure with an open, gaping mouth. It is grotesque in its silent vigil. Its malformed face is frozen in an eternal stony grimace, for it is a gargoyle. An impish figure from the Middle Ages, half human and half animal, it is a reminder of the lower, bestial side of human nature.

In Gothic art, one rarely finds a totally freestanding, isolated figure without an overhead canopy -- save the gargoyles. They jut out in splendid isolation both to fulfill their original purpose as rain gutters and to symbolize their rejection by the church.[1]

They also make a fitting symbol for the sin of anger. Most of us, when we were children, terrorized others with our share of temper tantrums. Enraged and frustrated, we would contort our faces into such horrible shapes, that some adult would mockingly warn us: "Be careful, or you may get stuck that way!"

They said it in jest, perhaps trying to dispel the temporary insanity of our fit. Little did they know, however, the ominous truth behind their words. For the fire of anger can bake the human heart until it becomes stone. If, indeed, we remain angry long enough, it is quite possible that our hearts will become petrified in the likeness of a hideous gargoyle. This is precisely where the greatest danger lies.

When I was a Boy Scout, I learned something very important about the nature of fire. I learned that three elements had to come together in order to make combustion possible, namely: air, fuel, and heat. The same can be said for anger. In this case, the air is represented by one's view of reality; the fuel by a list of grievances or grudges; and the heat by the actual offensive incidents that ignite the fire.

Anger is a response to a hurt or wound in the soul. In Naomi's case, the offending sparks that began the blaze were

19

famine, death and poverty. Nothing to be taken lightly! Some would even say that she had every right to be angry. She was furious at God and frustrated by the way her life had turned out. Bitterness and self-pity had moved in, sending thankfulness and joy packing.

> *Three elements to make fire (anger):*
> *1. air (distorted perspective)*
> *2. fuel (grudges)*
> *3. heat (offensive incidents)*

To make matters worse, Naomi's skewed view of reality acted like the Santa Ana winds in Southern California, which can turn a small grass fire into a raging inferno. Yes, she had lost her home in Israel. Yes, she had lost her husband and two sons. Yes, she was now destitute. But, that was not the whole story.

Bitterness so concentrates the mind that Naomi's loss was all she could see. She didn't consider the fact that God had saved her from the disease that had killed her family. She forgot to thank him for the gift of life and intelligence and even food during the famine. Finally, Naomi was so blinded by her anger that she could not see the greatest blessing God had given her -- Ruth. She looked the very key to her future happiness in the face and asked her to leave!

Picture this scene for a moment. Naomi returns to Bethlehem after more than ten years with nothing but a sack on her back and a foreigner as a companion. The long journey has left both women in rags, their skin red from exposure to the elements. Then someone recognizes her and word begins to spread throughout the tiny village. Her old friends, drawing water at the well, hear the news and drop their buckets. They rush immediately to the two strangers and exclaim, "Can this be Naomi?" Then, with Ruth standing right next to her, she says, "Don't call me Naomi (pleasant). Call me Mara (bitter), because the Almighty has made my life very bitter. I went away full, but the Lord has brought me back empty."[2] Have you ever considered how this statement might have made Ruth feel? I can imagine her thinking to herself, "What am I, chopped liver?"

Now, think for a moment. Is Naomi's complaint really true? Of course not! God did not want to destroy her; he wanted to bless her. As we discover at the end of the story, he had a plan to bring both of these ladies into the royal lineage of David, and hence, the Messiah. His purpose was not shame, disgrace and poverty, but rather, the highest honor a mere mortal could receive.

Naomi's problem was that she thought she was the main character in the story! She thought she was in the Book of Naomi, not the Book of Ruth. This is a big reason why some people struggle so mightily with anger and bitterness. Those who always place themselves at center stage tend to take everything that happens personally.

As long as we filter all events through the narrow lens of "How This Affects Me," bitterness will become a familiar companion. However, if we can learn to see the bigger picture, if we can begin to approximate God's point of view, much of the energy fanning the flames will subside. The ability to realize that, in so many cases, we play only a supporting role, requires humility which is derived from faith.

Fortunately, subsequent events reveal a change in Naomi, which leads me to believe that she overcame the deadly sin of anger. Speaking about the child to whom Ruth eventually gives birth, the women in the story, who function like the chorus in a Greek play, say to Naomi:

Praise be to the Lord, who this day has not left you without a kinsman-redeemer. May he become famous throughout Israel! He will renew your life and sustain you in your old age. For your daughter-in-law, who loves you and who is better to you than seven sons, has given him birth.[3]

We can surmise from these statements that Naomi came to realize that indeed, Ruth was not "chopped liver" but a wonderful blessing given to her by God. Her changed perspective sucked the very oxygen out of this fire of anger.

THE FIRE EXTINGUISHER OF PERSPECTIVE

Several years ago, I started a ministry to Chinese immigrants in Houston, Texas, that still continues to this day. In the beginning, it was very difficult to persuade people to underwrite such an endeavor. Therefore, I was forced to work at other jobs to support my family and the ministry as well. No one, it seemed, was interested.

After some fruitless calls and visits, I finally found a pastor who showed some interest in what we were doing. He was an old acquaintance and, after about six months of phone calls, letters and personal visits, I was at last able to secure a speaking engagement at his church on a Wednesday evening. I was excited about this opportunity and prepared carefully for it.

Now, my wife had left to spend the week with her sister who was having a baby. That meant that I had the responsibility of taking care of our two children, who were both quite young at the time. On the evening of the long-awaited service, I secured a babysitter for our daughter, who was about three years old. However, I decided to bring my seven-year-old son with me to the meeting, thinking he was old enough to behave properly. Boy, was that a mistake!

We had together agreed that he would stay with the other children during the service. Unfortunately, as I now know kids are wont to do, when the meeting began, he suddenly panicked and insisted on staying with me. Since it was too late to do anything else, I made him promise to sit quietly in his chair while I was preaching. (My second mistake of the night!) When it came time to do my thing, I walked up to the platform, leaving my angelic boy sitting in the congregation. The only "pulpit" they had was one of those flimsy music stands, which I carefully adjusted so I could see my notes.

Everything was going fine until I noticed that the music stand began to wobble a bit. It did it again, and I had to catch it before it crashed to the ground! I looked down and there was my beloved son, at my feet, rocking the stand. I continued preaching and then did what any loving parent would do: I slowly lifted my foot, placed it on his hand, and began to grind it into the floor with as much strength as I could muster! After a moment of doing this, I saw him out of the corner of my eye take his hand out, face contorted in a silent scream, and shake it from the pain I had inflicted.

All this time, I was still preaching, (wearing a forced smile) when the little fellow disappeared. I thought smugly, "Now that's the end of that: problem solved." As I continued my message, I soon noticed the eyes of the congregation, and they were no longer looking at me! Instead, they were focused behind me and off to the left. Some of them had their hands on their mouths, obviously trying to stifle an uncontrollable desire to laugh. I knew by this time that I had lost my audience completely, so I stopped preaching and followed everyone's gaze, which came to rest on my son, now standing behind me on the stage. I never actually found out what he had been doing to attract so much attention, but it was obvious that one of us had to go, and it wasn't going to be me! I grabbed his arm and gave him to the pastor, who took him out of the room. I finished my message and then, after the required pleasantries, we left.

Needless to say, I was furious when we got in the car! As I explained to Chris how disappointed I was, after all those months it took to get this service, he started to cry. Then, I cried a little myself. There we were, two dejected fellows going down the highway.

Within a few minutes I came to my senses. Of course, it wasn't Chris' fault; he was only a little boy. Instead, it was my wife who was to blame! She shouldn't have left me with these kids at such an important time. For a good while, my anger fluttered around like a parakeet looking for a place to land (why did my wife's sister have to have a baby *now*?), until finally the finger pointed at me. I knew that, actually, it was all my fault; however, that still didn't help my anger.

A few days later, when my wife returned home, she confessed that, the night I had called her about the fiasco, she had listened sympathetically while I vented my frustration, but had burst out laughing as soon as she hung up the phone. Then, she told her sister and brother-in-law, and they laughed even harder. In response, I sniffed, "Well, I'm glad that I provided some amusement for the three of you."

> ## Humor is one of the best fire extinguishers for anger.

Her comment, however, gradually began to change my perspective on the whole thing. The idea that some people could actually find this funny challenged my view of the situation. It took a day or two, but I felt my anger beginning to dissipate with the first chuckle that made its way up my windpipe.

Humor (which is nothing more than a changed perspective) is one of the best fire extinguishers for anger. It is absolutely impossible to laugh and remain angry -- as long as the laughter is genuine. Sarcastic, mean-spirited humor does not help. Only a good belly laugh (preferably at yourself) will do the trick.

Let's be careful here not to lose the point. As long as I focused narrowly on how all of this affected me, as long as I felt that the whole universe was conspiring to keep me from becoming successful, I was trapped in my bitterness. But when I took a step back and gained a more objective viewpoint, the anger disappeared.

THE BULLDOZER OF FORGIVENESS

If, in fact, one's distorted view of reality provides the oxygen for anger, then the fuel is most certainly our propensity to hold grudges and rehearse over and over again the wrongs (real or imagined) done to us. In 1971, Judith Wallerstein began a study of 131 children and adolescents and their divorcing parents from sixty families in Marin County, California.[4] The researchers interviewed all family members 18 months after the divorce. Five years later, they reinterviewed these same people. They did it again ten years later and then fifteen years. Amazingly, Wallerstein found that even after *ten years*, half of the women and one-third of the men in her study were still intensely angry at their former spouses. Carol Tavris comments:

One of the clearest contributions to lasting anger was that now-familiar factor: the rehearsal of grievances. The angry couples in Wallerstein's study talked incessantly to everyone they knew -- their children, friends, lawyers -- about the horrible sins of the former spouse. Wallerstein found, along with so many other psychologists, that this chorus of complaints does not diminish anger. On the contrary, she says, 'it is refueled with each incantation of sins.'[5]

The idiom, "to nurse grudges" is extremely revealing. I can picture in my mind a hospital room full of beds containing the hurts and wounds of the past. In one bed lies "a miserable childhood," in another, "a friend's betrayal" and half a dozen other causes of anger and bitterness from the past. All of these grudges are sick and slowly wasting away. Left alone and ignored, they will eventually expire. Yet, if we nurse them back to health, they can develop a strength and tenacity which is almost impossible to break. If we nurse them too well, these pathetic grudges will become our worst demons.

They provide the fuel for the fire. We have all known intensely angry people. At almost any family reunion there is at least one person that everyone treats with kid gloves. They walk

25

on eggshells lest they say the wrong thing that will set this individual off. The reason such personalities exist is due to the fact that their hearts are cluttered with so many flammable grudges that the smallest offense can set off a virtual forest fire. The deadly sin of anger makes us easily offended.

Every year in California and on the West Coast, forest fires rage out of control. I have always admired the fire fighters who risk their lives attempting to keep Mother Nature in check. One of the things they do is create "fire breaks," and one of the best tools for this is a bulldozer. That powerful, earth moving machine can come in and within minutes clear the ground of all combustible material. By the time the fire reaches that area, there is nothing left to burn. So it is with the "bulldozer of forgiveness."

Forgiveness, like nothing else, brings spiritual freedom. When we forgive others, their sin ceases to imprison us. When we receive forgiveness, our self-imposed exile is over. The garbage is cleaned away, the grudges die and the fire goes out.

Part Two

ENVY

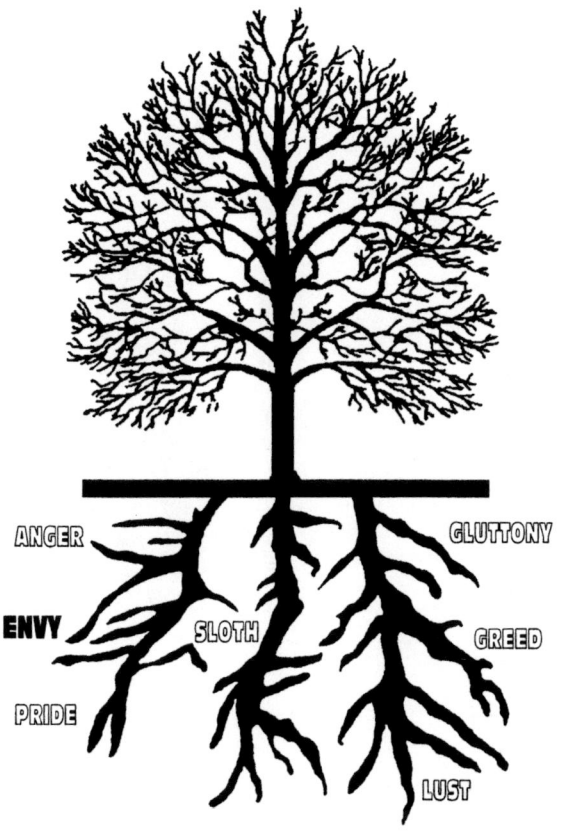

ENVY: Displeasure at another's success caused by a fear of insignificance.

THE SECURITY OF FAITH: Empowers us to be the unique human beings God created us to be.

A WITCH AND A KING

The king's hand trembled as he reached to knock on the witch's door. "That young upstart!" he fumed to himself. "This is all his fault. How humiliating to be reduced to this!"

A voice called from within. "Who is it?" It was a faint, creaky voice full of dust and decay.

"One who seeks direction," he replied. "I have come for advice." Even as he said the words, he felt a chill and pulled his cloak tighter to himself.

But the woman said, "Surely you know what the king would do. He has cut off all wizards and mediums from the land. You are setting a trap for me!"

"On my word, I am not," he replied. "I promise that no harm will come to you."

She opened the door and a foul odor filled his nostrils. It smelled of mildew and must. He hurried in, quickly sidestepping a broken floor board. What a place it was! Jars of every kind, containing only God knew what, lined the walls. On the fire was a pot of some unnamable substance that proved to be the source of the odor.

"Where can we talk?" he asked.

"Come into this back room. It will be safe there."

A sense of remorse came over him as he followed her. Why had he taken that shepherd into his court? After all he had done for him, this was his reward?

His mind went back to that first day they had met on the battlefield. For forty days, the enemy's greatest warrior had come out to the middle of the plain and taunted them. He was over nine feet tall and wore so much armor that no arrow could penetrate it.

Then, someone told him that a volunteer had actually agreed to fight the giant! He was expecting it to be Lachish or Jeshiah or one of the other seasoned heroes in Israel's army.

"Finally," he thought, "someone has lost their patience with this Philistine dog."

A short, ruddy boy tapped him on the shoulder.

"What is it?" he demanded, "Can't you see I am busy? Abner! Where is this 'volunteer'?"

"It is me, your majesty," replied the young boy with a polite bow. "I will defeat the Philistine."

He stared at him in disbelief. "Is this a joke?" He quickly pulled out his sword, and as he did, Abner and the other men standing nearby rushed to his side.

"No, your majesty! This is the man who volunteered to face the giant."

His face softened a bit and then broke into a howl of laughter. "Great! Wonderful! Now we are sending children out to fight our battles. I suppose next you will be telling me a whole regiment of old women are on their way!"

"Your majesty, please," the young boy protested. "I have been a shepherd watching my father's sheep. When a lion or a bear came and carried off one of the lambs, I went after it, struck it and rescued the sheep from its mouth. When it turned on me, I seized it by its hair and killed it.

"Your servant has killed both the lion and the bear, and this uncircumcised fool will be like one of them because he has defied the armies of the living God. The Lord who delivered me from the paw of the lion and the paw of the bear will deliver me from the hand of this man."

"Yes, I let him fight the giant," Saul now thought to himself. "I even offered my own armor to protect him, but he refused. It was the worst mistake of my life. How could I have known he would be so lucky? After he won the battle, people couldn't stop talking about him. Why, they even gave him greater glory than they gave to me! What a fool I was!

"Then, to invite him to be part of the palace household -- I must have been insane! Why couldn't I see what was happening? I trusted him as my son. I even gave him my daughter to marry, and this is how he repays me. From that first day I met him, he has done nothing but look for ways to undermine my authority and steal the kingdom away from me. He has even turned God against me so that I am forced to consult with this 'thing.'"

The witch seemed to read his thoughts. She looked at him suspiciously. "Just who are you, anyway?" she asked.

"That doesn't matter now. I need to talk to the spirits."

The message from the "other side" was not encouraging. It predicted his failure in battle the next day, the death of his son, Jonathan, and even his own demise.

The worst prediction by far, though, was that the kingdom would be torn out of his hands and given to that upstart, that traitor! Even now, at the end of his life, the name that had haunted him for so many years, the name he had tried to erase from the memory of every Israelite would live for ever, his nemesis: David!

THE BLACK RAVEN OF ENVY

*Once upon a midnight dreary, while I pondered, weak
    and weary,
Over many a quaint and curious volume of forgotten
    lore...*[1]

So begins Poe's famous poem, "The Raven." Like much
of his work, it is dark and depressing. When I first read it as a
young man, it sent chills up and down my spine. Then, when I
learned of the author's tragic life, I read it again and was
impressed by three emotions that strike the reader so forcefully.
The first was fear. When he hears the tapping and goes to open
the door only to find darkness, he stands there:

*Deep into that darkness peering, long I stood there
    wondering, fearing,
Doubting, dreaming dreams no mortals ever dared
    dream before.*

The fear is palpable throughout. As the poem continues, the
reader senses an insanity creeping in; a madness that defies
explanation. Finally, at the end, is despair:

*And the Raven, never flitting, still is sitting, still is
    sitting
On the pallid bust of Pallas just above my chamber
    door;
And his eyes have all the seeming of a demon's that is
    dreaming,
And the lamp-light o'er him streaming throws his
    shadow on the floor;
And my soul from out that shadow that lies floating on
    the floor*
                              Shall be lifted -- nevermore!

Fear, insanity and despair are the natural products of envy. The origin of Saul's envious relationship with David began when the women met the king, singing:

Saul has slain his thousands,
and David his tens of thousands.[2]

A FEAR OF BEING REPLACED

Thus, envy began, as it so often does, with a fear of being replaced. His position was in jeopardy, or so he thought. Saul said to himself, "What more can he get but the kingdom?" Here was a very insecure leader. He reminds me of people who have achieved positions of influence, positions of great leadership, perhaps through devious means. In their hearts they know they do not deserve such positions and they are terrified that someone else will discover it. They spend their days and nights covering their tracks and putting up a brave front lest anyone know the real person beneath. Often they project an air of confidence, but just below the surface lies a fear of failure, a dread of someone else replacing them.

> Truly great men and women do not fear being replaced, because they are only concerned with getting the job done.

What a contrast between King Saul and his son, Jonathan! If anyone should have felt threatened, it would have been the prince. After all, he was next in line to be king, and yet, there is not a trace of rivalry or competition. Instead of shunning him, Jonathan reached out to David and became his friend -- one of the most noble actions in the entire Bible. Jonathan reveals his greatness of soul, his total lack of the pettiness and jealousies that ruined his father.

Truly great men and women do not fear being replaced, because they are only concerned with getting the job done. If someone else can do it better, they would say, then let's help them succeed. Jonathan recognized that David was the man of the hour, and, like John the Baptist in the New Testament, could just as well have said, "He must increase, and I must decrease."

A FEAR OF BEING OUTDONE

Envy is also a fear of being outdone. A few years ago, a story surfaced in the news media here in Houston that shocked everyone in the city. It seems that there was a young, married couple who had some problems in their relationship (to put it mildly). The wife had a better job than the husband and, as a result, made more money than he did. The man's envy tormented him. What kind of a husband was he? How could she respect him if she were more successful?

One night, he couldn't take it any longer. He walked into the room with a shotgun where his wife was sitting and actually shot her several times in both legs! The damage was so severe that both mutilated limbs had to be amputated. What insanity! Envy is not merely content in wishing to have what the other person has. Instead, it goes a step further. Envy must also take away from and destroy the envied party.

A FEAR OF INSIGNIFICANCE

If we were to boil this sin down to its essence, I would have to say that it is a fear of insignificance. Does my life matter? Am I important?

When I was 20 years old, I took my first trip to Europe as a missionary. I worked with an organization called Open Doors which smuggled Bibles into what was then Communist Eastern Europe. It was a wonderful summer that led, a year later, to full time work with the mission. However, when I returned that fall to my home town, I had an experience that taught me something about this issue of significance.

It was my first Sunday back home, and I went to visit my home church, which had been instrumental in sending me to Europe in the first place. I was rather proud of my accomplishment and anticipated lots of pats on the back and warm welcomes. As I entered the sanctuary, I decided to sit near the front, because surely the pastor would want me to come to the pulpit and say a few words. I planned it all very carefully. I even sat on the end of the pew so I wouldn't disturb anyone when I got up to speak. Well, the service started and everything seemed to be going well. I know the pastor saw me, but nothing apparently registered. Not only did he not recognize me before the congregation, but when the time came to welcome the visitors, guess who got a visitor's card!

As I stuffed the card into my pocket, I had to chuckle a bit. Then, a powerful truth hit me: My significance does not depend upon what anyone else thinks -- Period! This truth has encouraged me many times in my ministry. We all do good things that no one else sees. Things for which we will never be rewarded, and even things for which we are sometimes misunderstood. However, the true servant of Jesus Christ is only concerned with pleasing One Person, and One alone.

King Saul was what Robert McGee would call an "approval addict."[3] His own insecurities as a leader led him to sin and rebel against God rather than risk the disapproval of his followers. He needed constant affirmation by those around him, and when he didn't get it, he responded with vicious attacks and fits of rage. His envy produced feelings of fear, insanity and despair. Consulting with the witch of Endor evidences the pathetic depths to which Saul had sunk. Proverbs 14:30 would have made an appropriate inscription for his headstone: "A heart at peace gives life to the body, but envy rots the bones."

THE SECURITY OF FAITH

In some respects, we who have only known life in a democracy may find it difficult to understand the ways of the kingdom of God. In a kingdom, there is only one vote that matters: that of the king. The people who inhabit his realm are not citizens with inalienable rights, but subjects expected to serve. Much of their destiny and place in society is predetermined by birth, not merit.

A king is not an equal opportunity employer, and neither is God! He distributes various talents to people according to his own wisdom and counsel. Some are born beautiful and intelligent while others are not. Some enjoy the fruits of freedom and economic opportunity while others slave away their entire lives imprisoned in poor, backward countries. Dissatisfaction with one's gifts (or lack thereof) is a seedbed for envy. If allowed to fester and grow, it will produce a poisonous crop, as in the case of King Saul. Rivals will be hated and resented rather than admired and emulated. This was a lesson I learned early in life.

When I was a young man, I had always wanted to build things with my hands. I relished wilderness activities and dreamed of one day building my own log cabin or birch bark canoe like the Indians. The only problem was, every time I tried to make something, it always turned out wrong. It was always crooked and never fit together very well. I just didn't have any natural ability with woodworking or mechanical devices.

> ## Only Americans wear
> ## lime green plaid leisure suits.

Then I went to Europe with the mission to which I alluded before. I had only been there about two weeks when an emergency occurred in Yugoslavia that required immediate attention. They sent another young man named Alan and me to pick up a vehicle that had broken down and return it to Holland. Alan was the same age as I (20 years old) and was also newly arrived from North America. We were given the director's own Mercedes Benz to drive across the continent for this mission. However, they said to us that two young men driving a Mercedes would look suspicious, so we should wear our suits. Well, the only suit I had (remember, this was the seventies) was a lime green leisure suit! To make matters worse, it was also plaid. When Alan (a Canadian) saw me, he said with some disgust, "Only Americans wear plaid!" That comment precipitated a kind of rivalry between us. Something inside of me rose up. I had to defend my national honor! How dare this Canadian insult an American! Throughout the trip, we went at it, sometimes good-naturedly, sometimes not. When we returned to Holland after being cooped up in the same car for two weeks, we didn't speak to each other for a while!

To add insult to injury, Alan was a marvel at mechanical devices. He could fix anything from electrical wiring to cesspools to cars. He had been raised on a farm, and things like that just seemed to come naturally to him. He became a mechanic at the mission and I worked in the office. However, I envied his abilities, and one day the opportunity came to prove myself. Alan had an old car he wanted to get rid of and offered to sell it to me for $25. He told me, "Everything works, except it needs a new battery and new brakes; the brakes are completely gone." Well, I bought the car and decided to fix the brakes myself. All of the staff were amazed when they saw me in overalls working on the car. Most people could have done the job in a day or two, but I think it took me about two weeks to finally figure it out and put on the new brakes. Then the day came for our victory ride. My new wife and I got into the car, and they pushed open the huge barn doors. All of the mission staff were there to cheer us on as I honked the horn and took off down the back pasture. The amazing thing was -- the brakes actually worked! However, we got a mile down the pasture when suddenly the car died. I tried and tried to get it started again, but nothing worked. Embarrassed, the two of us walked back to the mission in defeat, leaving the car in the pasture. As soon as we returned, I told Alan what had happened and he went down to the vehicle, got it started and drove it back! By that time, I was so disgusted with the whole thing, I told him to keep it!

After that experience, I began to reflect on why this was such a big deal to me. Why did it matter so much that I fix that car? What was I trying to prove?

In the introduction, we covered the point that faith gives us a secure identity. It is like a stationary lighthouse providing the ships with a point of reference for navigation. Though disoriented at times by the high waves and poor visibility, all the captain needs to do is find that beam of light which then directs him in the proper way.

My problem was that I had been listening to the "high waves" and "fog" of other people's expectations as to what a man should be. When it became obvious to me that I simply was not gifted in such ways, I had to trust that God had blessed me with gifts in other areas.

What a wonderful relief it was to know that I didn't have to be great at everything! Not only that, I could take another step and admire my good, Canadian friend and let him teach me a few things.

Envy, like all sin, can destroy a relationship. I am happy to say that after more than twenty years, Alan and I are still pals. He even called me from Canada on my 40th birthday and has invited us to visit his new home in the Canadian Rockies any time we want. What a terrible thing it would have been if I had allowed envy to ruin what has become a wonderful friendship.

> **He sees us in our most craven moments and in our most glorious, when we are selfish and petty and also heroic.**

Developing a thankful heart is one of the best solutions for this sin of envy. The way to do it is to recognize that everything we have is a gift from God. Paul's teaching about the body of Christ in I Corinthians 12 is especially helpful. He reminds us that we all have different gifts and different functions. One person is an eye, another is an ear and so on. Such an understanding will bring great peace and security to the soul, fortifying it against envious thoughts. The unique, special person you were created to be is a gift from God and cause for daily thanksgiving. You know you are free from envy when you can admire those who are more gifted and learn from them. When Saul and Jonathan looked at David, one saw a potential threat;

the other, a friend. The difference was Jonathan's thankful heart.

Thoreau said, "If a man does not keep pace with his companions, perhaps it is because he hears a different drummer. Let him step to the music which he hears, however measured or far away."[4] I have always felt that statement to be a great description of the Christian life. For to be a Christian means to be a misfit in this world, an outsider -- one who refuses to measure success by materialistic standards. Rather, the Lord Jesus pounds out a very different beat that tells us that the way up is down and the first shall be last. Let him who has the courage march to that music.

AN AUDIENCE OF ONE[5]

Soren Kierkegaard was a Danish philosopher who lived in the 19th century. Though he was a passionate Christian, he was also a biting and perceptive critic of the Danish church. He once condemned a very common idea of what happens during a worship service. He said that when the average person goes to church, he thinks of the pastor as the performer and the people as the audience. Not so! The truth of the matter, said Kierkegaard, is that the people are the performers, and the pastor is the prompter who stands behind the curtains helping them remember their lines. The silent and unseen audience is God who watches the congregation render its worship and prayers. That is such a profound truth, not just about church, but about the whole of our lives. We really do live for an audience of One. He sees us in our most craven moments and in our most glorious, when we are selfish and petty and also heroic.

He knows all of those unrequited acts of love, silent sufferings in the face of evil, and hidden deeds of unselfishness. Though no one else has ever recognized you for it, God is keeping records, and even a cup of cold water given in his name will not go unrewarded. Perhaps the best way to defeat envy is to realize that we are not in competition with one another for our Father's affection. We can rest in his love and unconditional acceptance.

Part Three

PRIDE

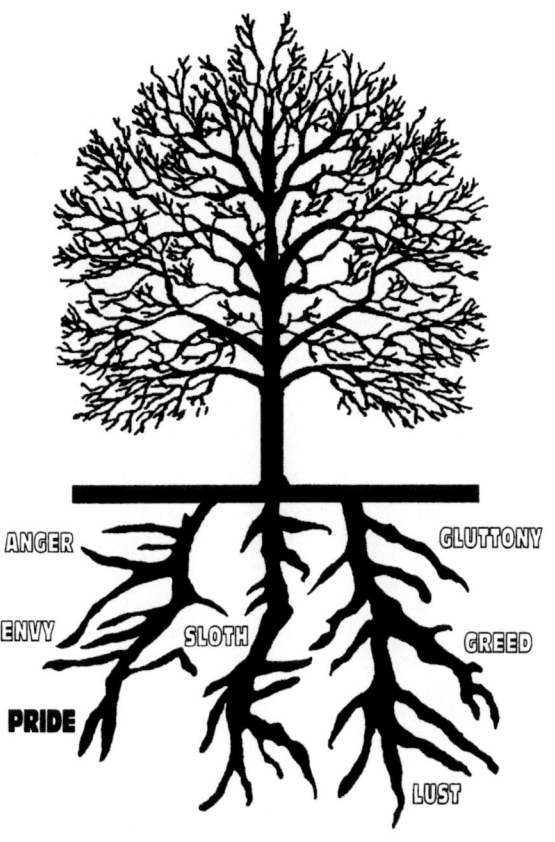

PRIDE: An overly high opinion of oneself resulting in a condescending disdain for others.

THE EXPERIENCE OF FAITH: Overwhelms us with the majesty of God in such a way that we become self-forgetful.

THE PROPHET BIGOT

He awoke with great spasms of coughing and gasping for oxygen. Quickly, though, his relief at breathing turned to nausea as the putrid air filled his nostrils. "Where am I?" he thought, as he peered into the darkness around him. He was against a wall, but not like any other wall he'd ever felt. It was wet and spongy, irregularly shaped. The entire room seemed to be in motion, and it gave him a sickly feeling, like being on a ship in the middle of a storm.

Then he remembered. The guilt came rushing back. Why hadn't he just stayed home? It seemed he was always making bad decisions -- decisions that, even as he made them, he regretted. How could he have imagined that he could get away with it? He should have known better. And now, he was going to pay the ultimate price.

His thoughts were interrupted by a fierce burning sensation on his right leg. He cried out in pain and instinctively curled up like a ball. What could that be? It felt like the sting of salt water on sunburned skin. The pain was incredible.

"It's all their fault!" he thought bitterly. "None of this would have happened had it not been for those pagan devil worshippers! How can they live the way they do? And so cruel!" He shuddered at the memory of the tales he had heard of Assyrian torture. "I would sooner be dead than to do anything on their behalf.

"What's the use? I'm all alone now, so I must figure a way to get out of this mess. Perhaps if I could start a fire, I could at least get my bearings." He began to feel around in the darkness. Everything that he touched seemed saturated with water. "No hope of a fire here."

Suddenly, the faint glimmer of a light appeared. It was not clear at all, but diffuse and pale. He couldn't tell where it was coming from, but the silence was suddenly broken by a loud, roaring sound. He had heard that sound before -- on the beach! He had just enough time to take a deep breath before waves of seawater overwhelmed him and tossed his body back

43

and forth. It seemed like an eternity before he could get back to the air.

As he crawled halfway out of the water, his head was wrapped in something cold and sticky. He pulled at it frantically, then realized, "It's only seaweed." All around him, he could feel small creatures wriggling and jumping. As he climbed up higher to his old dry spot, it dawned on him that the waves had brought in a school of fish. "Well, at least I won't starve."

Then he remembered the events of the past few days. Buying a ticket on the boat to Tarshish, the great storm at sea, and the terror in the eyes of the sailors. He remembered how they cast lots to discover who was to blame for their predicament, and how he had been the one singled out. Reluctantly, he had said to them, "Throw me overboard and the storm will cease."

To their credit, they refused to do this, hoping for another solution. Yet, as the storm became more intense, they cried out to God, "Please do not hold us accountable for the blood of the innocent." Then, as one man, they picked him up and threw him into the water. That was the last thing he remembered until he woke up in this wet, slimy room.

Regret came flooding back into his mind like the previous waves. "Why does everything have to be hard for me? Just once, I'd like to be the nice guy, the one everybody likes. I only see things in black and white; that is my curse. No compromise, no middle ground with me, no mercy. I should learn to be more patient. I know I'm hard to live with. Yet, it seems when I'm on the verge of saying something good it comes out all wrong. -- What now?"

His thoughts were interrupted again as he felt the room sinking lower and lower. It was similar to falling, yet different, like sinking into quicksand. The air seemed to be getting colder and darker. It was if he were tunneling down to the very roots of the mountains. A great weight grew heavier with each passing moment. A feeling of doom came over him. He realized now with horror where he was. Inside the belly of a whale!

44

THE SIBERIAN WINTER OF PRIDE

Botany Bay, Patmos and Siberia -- all places of exile, all places of silence. When I think of Siberia, I imagine the stillness of the snow falling, muffling all sound. I contemplate the fate of political prisoners from Dostoyevsky to Solzhenitsyn, made mute by their consciences. I picture English criminals, taciturn and morose, arriving in Australia, the continent at the end of the world. Then there is the isle of Patmos with the lonely Apostle John looking out across the vast Mediterranean and foreseeing a heaven in which there is no more sea. All places of exile, all places of silence.

ALOOF ARROGANCE

Pride is a self-imposed exile from God and others. One of the most striking things about Jonah was his singular isolation. As Donald Capps noted in his book, Jonah was a stranger on the boat, a stranger in the city of Ninevah and even, as we read in chapter four of the book of Jonah, a stranger to God.[1] Nowhere, however, is Jonah's lonely exile more acute than in the belly of the whale. What a picture of the prison house of pride! How many domestic squabbles and even wars can be attributed to this evil? Pride is one of the most damaging of sins to human relationships, due to its alienating power.

In his study of four hundred years of charity work in North America, Professor Marvin Olasky devotes a chapter to what he calls "the Seven Marks of Compassion."[2] When a person in the 19th century came to a charity seeking help, the very first question that was asked was, "Where is your family?" This was the first "mark" of compassion that began with an "A" for *association*. Christian workers understood that one of the most common reasons people became poor was that in one way or another, they had become estranged from their families. Young runaways, derelict fathers and the elderly who had lost contact with their relatives were the typical cases. (They still

45

are.) Every effort was made to re-establish the family ties that had been broken.

Far too often, the culprit responsible for those broken relationships is the sin of pride. Like Jonah in chapter four, the proud person marches off to sulk, carefully nursing his real or imagined grievances. Some people have become homeless because they would rather live on the street than ask their family for help. In cases like this, charity workers would attempt to "re-connect" this person with either a church or synagogue or get them involved in some kind of human society. In order for their efforts to succeed, however, a certain degree of humility in the "client" was essential.

> Hell, if it is anything, is a place of eternal loneliness.
> Without the moderating restraints of humility,
> the regions of Hades will suffer from raw, naked pride.

This brings us to the crux of the problem. The proud person is under the delusion that he does not need others. He can go it alone. Was this not the sin of Satan and even Adam and Eve? How appropriate that God's punishment for humanity's pride was exile from the garden of Eden. Hell, if it is anything, is a place of eternal loneliness. Without the moderating restraints of humility, the regions of Hades will suffer from raw, naked pride, which makes relationships of any kind impossible.

On earth, however, there is still hope. Cut off from human companionship, Jonah does the first positive thing in the book: he prays. The isolation of sin causes us, like the ancient prophet, to cry out to God for help and mercy.

TERMINAL BIGOTRY

The prophet is quite candid about his reasons for refusing the Lord's command to go to Ninevah. In chapter four, he says that he knew that by preaching to the Ninevites, Israel's implacable, cruel enemies, he was opening the possibility of their salvation. There was no compassion or concern at all in Jonah's heart.

His reluctance to go to Ninevah and his utter contempt and disregard for its welfare seems to be a case of terminal bigotry. Although this problem has garnered a great deal of attention in our modern, multicultural world, the roots of these sins are poorly understood. Take, for example, the 1960s musical, *South Pacific*. In the story, there are two white Americans, a man and a woman, who each love a person of another race or nationality. They both have reservations about marrying these people. In the case of the man, he loves a Tonkanese girl, while the woman loves a Frenchman. Her real problem, though, is that this Frenchman has been married to a native woman (now deceased). She bore him two children who, of course, were of mixed blood. The song that the American man sings to the American woman is "You've Got To Be Carefully Taught." The message is that children must be taught how to hate and have prejudice for others.

While this is a popular idea and one of the cardinal myths of humanism, nothing could be further from the truth. I was once a child and I also have children of my own. In fact, I have known quite a few children in my lifetime, and I would say that the truth is the exact opposite of the song from South Pacific. Children must be carefully taught *not* to harbor prejudice, bigotry and contempt for others who are not like themselves.

The hard truth is that these sins are outgrowths of the sin of pride which is found in every human heart. All people, in a moment of honesty, will confess that there have been times in which they shrunk back or avoided someone who was handicapped, or told unkind jokes about a person of another race, or even deliberately belittled someone who was different.

Bigotry, in a sick kind of way, makes us feel better about ourselves. Even the word itself goes back to Old French. *Bigot* was a pejorative term the French had for the Normans! In every country I have visited or lived in, one will always find a unique assortment of prejudices. In Holland, I discovered that the Dutch looked down on the Belgians. The Germans despised the

Polish, while the Polish made fun of the Russians! In Washington State I often heard disparaging remarks about race relations in the American South, but then the very same person would complain about Canadians or Asians! Also, among the Chinese there is great prejudice between those who live in the cities and the "peasants" inhabiting the countryside. The point is that we often develop our strongest prejudices about people who live near us but are different from us.

Perhaps this explains the failure of integration to solve our race problems in the United States. The hope was that if we could just integrate the public schools, then everyone would learn to appreciate each other and racial harmony would break out across the country. Thirty years later, even the most vocal proponents of integration will admit that the problems of race seem as intractable as ever.[3]

From the Christian point of view, these problems are not so mysterious. As long as human beings exist, pride and prejudice will continue. The solution does not lie with the government or social programs. It can only be healed by a work of grace in each individual's heart.

CRITICAL CYNICISM

Aloof arrogance and terminal bigotry naturally produce critical cynicism. The word itself can be traced back to the ancient Greek philosophers known as the Cynics, the most famous of whom was Diogenes. His philosophy was that people should live "according to nature." He saw society as positively artificial, and the true Cynic would stand aloof from all such entanglements. He was the original hippie, clothed in rags and disdainful of the plastic society of manners, morals, and materialism. The most famous legend about Diogenes is that one day, Alexander the Great paid a visit. The old ragged philosopher had made a home out of a wine crate and was lying in the sunshine when the famous conqueror came calling. After speaking with him at length, Alexander is reputed to have said, "Diogenes, I will give you anything you request from my empire." Diogenes responded, "My one request, Alexander, is that you move out of my sunlight."

It was Diogenes who once lit a lantern and roamed the city streets in search of an honest man. Of course, he did not find one. Cynics never do. They derive their greatest joy from sitting back and watching others, who are sincerely trying to do something, make mistakes. Of these three fruits of pride, cynicism is perhaps the most difficult to overcome.

In Jonah's case, we are left to wonder if he ever recovered from this occupational hazard of the ministry. It is easy for preachers and prophets to become cynical. There is a fine line between motivation and manipulation when it comes to preaching sermons or announcing the judgment of God upon a city. Jonah confesses that this was the very reason he fled from the presence of the Lord the first time. As he announced the fearful message, he wanted judgment, not mercy!

THE EXPERIENCE OF FAITH

The thesis of this book is that when we are born again, God drops within our hearts three powerful virtues, which are our greatest weapons against sin: faith, hope and love. We have seen how the perspective of faith can defeat anger and the security of faith can win over envy. Now, let's pull this together to examine how the experience of faith overcomes pride, which is the deepest root and wellspring of the other two sins.

Have you ever considered the question as to how one becomes humble? Harry Ironside once asked this of a friend.[4] He had been struggling with pride, and so his friend suggested a simple remedy. He told the famous and dignified pastor to write Bible verses on the front and back of a sandwich board, place it around his neck and spend the entire day walking through downtown Chicago. Well, he did it, and it certainly was a very humbling experience. However, as he returned home that evening, he thought to himself as he took off the sandwich board, "I wonder how many people would have done what I did today?" In the flash of a millisecond all the "humility" he had worked so hard to attain vanished. For that is precisely the

49

problem. Humility, like joy or happiness, is not an original thing. Instead, it is a by-product of something else. It cannot be sought and attained in its own right. It is a gift received by faith, a serendipitous grace created by an encounter with the living God.

True humility is not self-negation, it is not self-abasement, it is not self-loathing; it is self-forgetfulness.

The best way I can explain this is to consider what happens to us when we encounter a great work of art, whether it be a painting, beautiful music, a movie or a book. No matter what the case, when the observers are drawn into the art, they begin to lose all self-consciousness. They cease thinking about what kind of clothes they may be wearing or where they stand in the pecking order at work or what others might be thinking. Instead, they become absorbed in the art and, even if only for a few moments, forget that they are the center of the universe. That is exactly what happens to us when we truly worship God. We are drawn out of ourselves and are reminded that he is the center of all things and that we are simply tiny satellites that revolve around a gigantic sun.

True humility is not self-negation, it is not self-abasement, it is not self-loathing; it is self-forgetfulness. It is a direct result of faith, which reaches out in childlike fashion to an unseen God. The power of his "gravity" pulls us into his orbit and away from our puny attempts to create our own world. This is not unlike the sense of humility that comes over us while standing before some of the wonders of nature such as the Grand Canyon, feeling like a flea on the back of a cow. Or contemplating a giant redwood and knowing that it was a young sapling before Columbus discovered America. In comparison to these things, we are but passing tourists on this planet called earth. To look in the heavens at night and try to imagine the enormous distances to the nearest star. Then, to realize that

God is still greater than all these. This is what the Psalmist must have been doing when he wrote:

In the beginning you laid the foundations of the earth,
and the heavens are the work of your hands.
They will perish, but you remain;
they will all wear out like a garment.
Like clothing you will change them
and they will be discarded.
But you remain the same, and your years will never end.[5]

Humility toward God is developed through worship. Humility toward man is developed through fellowship. In both cases, faith is at work, destroying the walls of separation. The very act of attending church and bowing our heads in prayer is an acknowledgment that there exists Someone greater than ourselves. It also teaches us that we cannot live the Christian life alone. We need one another more than we realize.

THE FELLOWSHIP OF THE SAINTS

The experience of faith, which is the experience of God himself, defeats this deadly sin in another way as well. At the beginning of this chapter, pride was described as a kind of exile, a poison which ruins every relationship. The proud man refuses to admit his need of anything or anybody. This is the attitude which lies behind so much prejudice and "caste" differences in our world. The fellowship of the saints, which grows naturally out of the life of faith, is a marvelous antidote for this evil.

I had a friend in high school named Tom. This was in the mid-seventies at the tail end of the "Jesus Movement." There were ten or fifteen of us "Jesus freaks" who banded together in what was a sometimes hostile environment in our public school. Tom was a little different. He was tall and skinny, always carried a big Bible with him and wore a large cross around his neck. Often he dressed in black, which made him look like a priest. (He was fond of "blessing" people in the hallway with the sign of the cross, which only strengthened the

51

image.) American high school has got to be one of the most class conscious places on the face of the earth. Kids can be downright cruel to those who don't fit in, and Tom stuck out like a sore thumb. However, he was my brother in Christ and I have always felt that Christians should stick together. So we became friends.

As I got to know Tom, I discovered that he wasn't Catholic; instead, he belonged to the Salvation Army church. Somehow, he convinced me one Saturday evening to go with him on the "bar route." He explained to me that it was a tradition in the Salvation Army for representatives to visit all the bars in town selling the "War Cry" magazine to the patrons. It was both a way to be a witness and to raise money for the organization. Well, here we were, two seventeen-year-old boys going from bar to bar. Tom was dressed in his Salvation Army uniform and he loaned me an official hat to wear. As you can imagine, we were not always warmly received by our prospects. We visited a gay bar in which one of the men told me he had just gotten out of prison. When I asked him (foolishly) why he had been incarcerated, he glowered at me and said, "Murder!" (At that point I motioned to Tom that this might be a good time to leave.) In another bar, an intoxicated customer grabbed my hat and started dancing around with it. As I stood there, getting red in the face, Tom graciously retrieved it for me. In fact, that night my respect for him increased dramatically. He had done this a few times before and conducted himself with grace and dignity. At the end of the night, we pulled our car up to a topless bar. As we sat in the parking lot, I said to Tom, "I don't think I can do this." We looked at one another, then looked at the gaudy neon lights and decided to call it a night!

The point of this story is that my life was deeply enriched through my Salvation Army buddy. I admired his intelligence and his decision to deliberately be different from everyone else. (That took guts in our high school!) I also enjoyed Tom's stories about the incredible history of the "Army" and its eccentric founder, General William Booth. If I had allowed pride to separate us, I would have missed a real blessing. This is what the life of faith forces us to do. The church is open to the public, and no matter their background, their race, their social status or their intelligence, we must show kindness, as Paul says, especially to the household of faith.[6] At the foot of the cross, we all stand on the same level.

Part Four

SLOTH

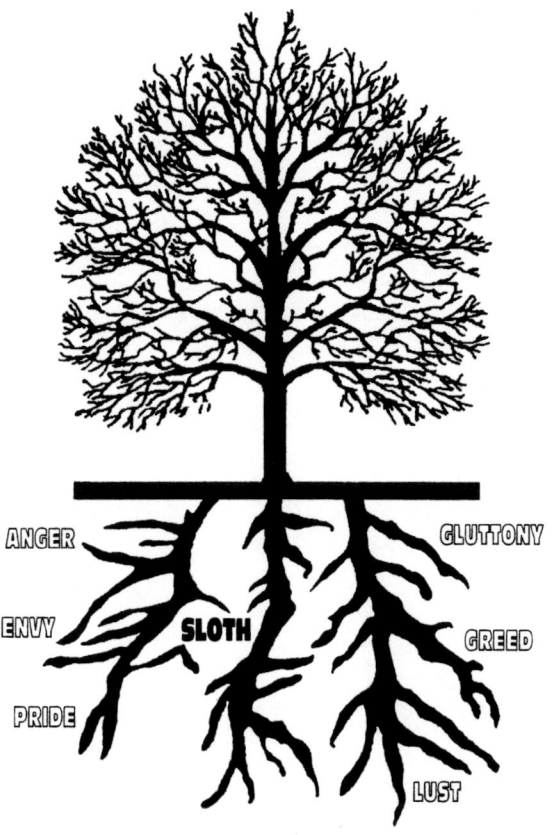

SLOTH: A state of indifference which leads to inactivity, boredom and despair.

THE ANTIOXIDANT OF HOPE: Purifies our soul by restoring to us a child-like sense of wonder and the ability to believe again in miracles.

THE DISILLUSIONED KING

The change had been gradual and slow. He remembered fondly how he had risen early every morning eager to begin the new day, his mind bursting with ideas for his many projects. He relished the planning sessions for the great new temple that was under construction. This building had been his father's dream, and now the son was able to see it through to completion. His eyes were misty as he watched the workmen placing the finishing touches on the magnificent structure. If only his father could be here today.

Years passed and many other projects were completed, one by one. His life could not have been more perfect. Wise men and scholars traveled from around the world to hear his teachings and marvel at the enormous reservoir of his knowledge. Kings even presented their daughters to him in marriage, thus solidifying the political ties that brought peace to his realm. Life was full, and every evening he enjoyed the sleep of accomplishment and satisfaction.

Tonight, however, was different. He had tossed and turned for hours in bed, unable to fall asleep. He decided to get up and call for one of his advisors. Zabud appeared a few minutes later, wiping sleep from his eyes. He was beginning to grow accustomed to these late night conferences, which were becoming more frequent.

Zabud bowed on one knee and waited for the king to speak, as was the custom. He could hear scrolls rattling and the absentminded mumbling of Solomon to himself. This went on for several minutes until he heard, "Ah, Zabud, my friend, please come up to my desk." That was his signal, and Zabud rose stiffly, hiding a yawn quickly with his hand.

"I'm sorry to disturb your sleep, but there are a few matters that I must discuss." He continued, "Here I am, the king of Israel. I have a beautiful palace, hundreds of gorgeous wives, my kingdom is at peace, and I may have whatever my heart desires.

"Compared to my father, my life is idyllic. Did I tell you that he once actually went to live with our enemies, the Philistines? He even fought with them in several campaigns before he became king. I see you are surprised; not many people know this. His life was one, long continuous battle. I was even told that one day, before I was born, your father, Nathan, came in and confronted him about his supposed adultery with my mother. Is that true, Zabud?"

Before he had a chance to answer, Solomon continued, "That doesn't matter now. In fact, nothing that we do seems to matter. Have you ever considered, my friend, the absolute futility of life?"

Zabud noticed a now familiar shadow fall across Solomon's face. It pained him to see his master in such a state. "Your majesty, may I speak with candor?"

"Please do."

"How can you consider all the great projects you have accomplished futile? The temple, this palace, and the peace and prosperity of Jerusalem are important both in the eyes of God and man. You have blessed the earth with your wisdom -- isn't that cause for satisfaction?"

"Yes, Zabud, one would think so, but I have found even wisdom to be a false mistress. The more wisdom I accumulate, the more sorrow and grief comes with it. I was far happier as an ignorant child." He paused, slumping down in his chair. Then -- "Meaningless!" cried the king, pounding his desk, "It is all utterly meaningless!"

Zabud was startled at his sudden outburst.

"Look, generations come and generations go, but the earth remains forever." He was pacing the floor now. "The sun rises and the sun sets, and hurries back to where it rises. The wind blows to the south and turns to the north; round and round it goes, ever returning on its course. All streams flow into the sea, yet the sea is never full. It is all an endless circle of futility.

"Who is to say what will happen after we die? This great temple I built, the wealth and prosperity of Jerusalem, how long will it last? Who is to say if the next king that follows me will be a wise man or a fool? Yet, he will have control over all that I have done. The more I consider these things, the more my heart begins to despair."

Zabud felt confused and not sure how to comfort his beloved master. He had always been intimidated by Solomon's superior intellect, but now all that knowledge seemed to fail him.

"Your majesty," he said, breaking the silence that had ensued, "I do believe there is a time for everything, and a purpose for every activity. Why, God has put eternity in the hearts of men, yet they cannot fathom the depths of his plan. . . . not even you." He spoke those last words with some trepidation. One does not criticize a king lightly!

Solomon did not seem to notice. Instead, he was remembering his younger days, when God seemed so close to him and so real. His faith had been simple then; now there were too many things to consider. He had studied the philosophies of the East and investigated the other religions of Egypt and the surrounding countries. His wives had told him charming fables and legends about their gods and goddesses. What was a man to think?

"Zabud," he said in a pensive tone of voice, "Do you suppose that there really is only one, true God? Sometimes I wonder if there is any God at all."

"Your majesty!" Zabud replied in a frightened whisper. "Don't say such things. Even in the middle of the night, God can hear every word."

"If that is true, I would like him to know that I am most displeased with him!" he said imperiously. "This rat's maze of an earth has become too wearisome for me. What is the meaning of it all? That's what I would like to know."

Solomon walked out to his balcony and gazed up at the stars.

Zabud was speechless. Never had he heard such thoughts spoken out loud. What was to become of this son of David?

After a long pause of silence, Solomon, still looking up at the stars, said, "Thank you, my friend, for listening. Please return to bed. We shall talk more about these things again."

Zabud placed his hand on the great man's shoulder. "I will pray for you tonight."

"Thank you," was all the king said.

THE RELENTLESS TERMITES
OF SLOTH

I live in Houston, Texas, an exciting, modern city. It is the headquarters of NASA, which is, one could argue, the most farsighted, futuristic organization in the world. From the famous Medical Center to the Astrodome to NASA, this city is clearly poised to remain a leader well into the 21st century. Yet, as I drive around, from time to time, a thought continues to nip at my brain. I wonder, how much of a victory have we really achieved over Mother Nature? The truth of the matter is that every minute of every day, nature does her best to sabotage our most heroic efforts. No one is more effective at doing that than the tiny termite. These ant-like creatures are very important in that they break down dead wood in forests and turn it into soil. They are actually one of the earth's most effective recyclers. Unfortunately, as every homeowner knows, houses are made out of dead wood, the termite's food supply. Once inside the woodwork of a building, they tunnel in all directions, with no openings showing from the outside. The first indication of their presence may well be the collapse of a wall or stairway. They work in large numbers, and as many as 4,000 have been counted in one cubic foot of wood!

Silently yet relentlessly, the termites work, doing their greatest damage unseen by human eyes. Of all the seven sins that we will examine in this book, sloth is definitely the most insidious, and, in some ways, the most destructive. Unlike gluttony or lust or greed, which can be quickly recognized, sloth comes in many disguises. It is more of an absence than a presence -- an emptiness that gnaws away at our resolve and calls into question our most deeply held beliefs. One of the earliest Christian writers on this subject called it the "noonday demon: who makes the sun appear sluggish and immobile, as if the day had fifty hours."[1] He added, "It is the most oppressive of all demons." Other early writers listed Judas as one of its casualties -- a man so overcome by remorse, depression and despair that suicide seemed the only answer.

Today, Christians sometimes refer to it as "spiritual dryness" or indifference concerning the things of God. It is without a doubt the greatest enemy of revival on either an individual or social level. Indeed, one could call it the "demon of the status quo."

> # Sloth slows down great enterprises and dreams, ruins gleaming cities and makes us old before our years.

Sloth is the source from which most of our sins of omission originate. The Greek word, *acedia*, which is translated as sloth, means literally, "not to care" or "lack of care." In English, we call it apathy. Dorothy Sayers caught the essence of this sin when she wrote, "It is the sin that believes in nothing, cares for nothing, seeks to know nothing, interferes with nothing, enjoys nothing, hates nothing, finds purpose in nothing, lives for nothing, and remains alive because there is nothing for which it will die."[2]

This is the sin that abets the natural law of entropy. It slows down great enterprises and dreams, ruins gleaming cities and makes us old before our years. It is the inertia that pulls at us every day, every hour, every minute. We have all felt its force. We have all heard it whispering in our ears to slow down.

Solomon evinced many of the symptoms of sloth, especially in the book of Ecclesiastes. He writes:

> *"Meaningless! Meaningless!" says the Teacher.*
> *"Utterly meaningless! Everything is meaningless!"*[3]

and then later in chapter two:

> *So I hated life, because the work that is done under the sun was grievous to me. All of it is meaningless, a*

chasing after the wind. I hated all the things I had toiled for under the sun, because I must leave them to the one who comes after me. And who knows whether he will be a wise man or a fool? Yet he will have control over all the work into which I have poured my effort and skill under the sun. This too is meaningless. So my heart began to despair over all my toilsome labor under the sun.[4]

There is an old Jewish tradition which says that Solomon in his youth wrote the beautiful love poems in the Song of Solomon. Then, as he embarked upon his life's work, he composed the practical wisdom of the Proverbs. Finally, as he grew old, he recorded the bitter findings of a disappointed and desperate old man whose endless pursuit for meaning and purpose in life "under the sun" had ended in futility.

It is curious, however, that Solomon, of all people, should have ended up with such a dim outlook. After all, his reign marked the golden age of the nation of Israel. It was during this time that the great temple was finally constructed and the ark of the covenant given a proper resting place. His was an extremely productive reign with many sterling accomplishments: a gorgeous palace in which to live, a throne inlaid with ivory, and the admiration and homage of kings and queens from around the world. In addition to all that, he was blessed with peace during his forty year tenure and enjoyed the attention of seven hundred wives and three hundred concubines. What more could a man ask for?

Consider Solomon's position for a moment. His kingdom is at peace, his great projects are behind him -- now what? From every possible worldly definition of success, Solomon had it. Perhaps that was his problem. Sometimes, success can become a more difficult adversary than failure. If we are not careful, we can be lulled into a state of apathy and spiritual laziness.

In some ways, it should not surprise us that Solomon had such a struggle with sloth, for in many respects, his situation parallels our own today. We live in a society which is also experiencing a "golden age" of impressive wealth and opportunity. Never before have people lived as comfortably as we do today. I can get into my car, no matter what the weather, and travel in complete comfort. Even during my trip I can choose to listen to one of dozens of radio stations, a cassette tape, or even a CD. When I arrive at my hotel, I can order room service, be entertained by the television and sleep in a comfortable bed. Diseases that once struck terror in man's heart can today be easily treated. Laborsaving devices from dishwashers to computers to weed eaters reduce the amount of time spent on irksome, repetitive tasks, leaving us free for more creative, meaningful endeavors.

By this time, we should all be Albert Einsteins by seizing upon the limitless opportunities available for self-improvement. Yet, perhaps never before have people been as bored as they are today. Boredom is the most common expression of the sin of sloth in the modern, western world. It is such an all-pervasive attitude that we have coined over 71 different words to express some aspect of it![5] Just as Eskimos need many words for snow, so do we when it comes to boredom.

TROUBLE DEFEATS BOREDOM

Hyrum Smith, founder and CEO of the Franklin Quest Co., tells an interesting story from his boyhood.

I grew up in Honolulu, and when I was eleven years old I decided I could swim across Hanauma Bay, on the southern tip of Oahu. It's a beautiful place, a mile and a quarter across, with water about eighty feet deep. I went there, dove into the water, and started to swim across. Well, the waves were quite big that day, and I couldn't see the other side. Halfway across, I started to drown. You get some interesting feelings when you think you're going to drown. I was treading water, facing out to sea, when all of a sudden I saw a fin gliding through the water about ten feet away. My need

*to get to the other side went absolutely crazy. What I
discovered about myself was this: It's okay to drown.
It's not okay to get eaten!* [6]

I believe Solomon was drowning in a sea of sloth. All of
his needs were met. Everything he could wish for was his.
Sloth can be a comfortable sin. Instead of continuing the
struggle, we give in to the soft side of life. We don't want to
leave our comfort zones, even if it means drowning.

Then come the "sharks" of trouble. No one likes them,
no one wants them. Yet, they come to everyone, and they are
sometimes the only thing that will awaken us from our apathetic
slumbers.

DREAMS DEFEAT SLOTH

I once knew a man at work who was the most negative,
apathetic person I have ever known. He almost never had a
good word to say. He was middle-aged, single and completely
self-centered. Yet, for some reason, we became friends. Even
after I left that job, we would have lunch together about once a
year. A few years later, I saw him again and he was a changed
man. He was excited about life, he had new energy and even his
face looked different. What had changed? He had taken up skin
diving! He traveled down to Mexico three and four times a year
to swim with the dolphins and enjoy the beach. He had finally
found something that really turned him on.

Nothing is sadder than a person who goes through life
completely bored. Find something that you can get excited
about! Sloth can never be defeated by attacking it directly.
Instead, a vision or dream must somehow be birthed inside that
will overwhelm this deadly sin. Solomon himself gave this
advice:

*Go to the ant, you sluggard; consider its ways and be wise!
It has no commander, no overseer or ruler,
yet it stores its provisions in summer and gathers its food at
harvest.* [7]

THE ANTIOXIDANT OF HOPE

"The mass of men lead lives of quiet desperation."[8]   So wrote Thoreau during his famous sojourn at Walden pond. It sounds as if he were describing King Solomon, doesn't it? We find him in Ecclesiastes desperately searching for a reason to live. As most Bible scholars will tell you, his problem is that he limits his observation to life *under* the sun. He has lost the connections to ultimate meaning. Thus, one finds references to the endless cycles of birth and death, war and peace, work and sleep. It is all so tiresome and boring. Sloth eats away at our hope like a termite, convincing us that nothing will ever change.

One phrase that I have learned to detest when sociologists and statisticians prognosticate about the future is "assuming present trends continue." This is the language of sloth. Hope shouts in reply, "Present trends will not continue, for we shall do something about it!"

Hope is not some gambler's expectation of uncertain riches. Rather, it is a powerful force that lifts our gaze "above the sun" to the source of our confidence and strength -- God himself. It is active and aggressive, clear-eyed and bold in asserting that God is for us, not against us.

Hope acts as an antioxidant of the soul. In recent years, medical science has begun to get a better understanding of the aging and disease processes of the body. They have learned that the daily pollution we are exposed to in our air, water and food produces something called "free radicals" which attack healthy cells. They cause our bodies to age faster and become more vulnerable to heart disease, cancer and stroke. Antioxidants, found in such vitamins as A, C and E, help reverse this degenerative process, neutralizing the free radicals before they do any damage.

In the same way, we live our entire lives in a heavily polluted moral and spiritual world. We are surrounded by rebellious attitudes and cynical dispositions which wear away and damage our ability to believe. If this process continues unabated, the end result can be fatal. We can lose two qualities that are especially effective in combating sloth: childlike innocence and a sense of wonder. Let's consider each of these for a moment.

We can never have absolute innocence restored to us. This was lost by Adam and Eve when they ate from the tree of the knowledge of good and evil. This knowledge is what destroyed their innocence. It is what destroys ours as well. The dictionary lists "ignorant" and "unaware" as secondary meanings for this word. Like a country bumpkin who gets cheated by the city slickers, it doesn't take long for us to "wise up" and learn the ways of the world. The trick is for the honest man to know about these things without making use of them himself. To become, in Jesus' words, "wise as serpents, yet harmless as doves." This is part of the majesty of redemption. Many Christian writers have noted that there is greater glory in redeemed man than in unfallen man. No, we will never know the absolute innocence of the Garden of Eden, but we can experience a restored version of it through the power of hope.

> # Hope pulls us forward
> # with a mounting sense of adventure,
> # even turning dread death
> # into a mere passageway
> # to a better, more exciting life.

I personally lost some of my innocence about the Bible when I went to seminary. Although I attended a theologically conservative school, I was exposed to many ideas that had never occurred to me. I learned about Wellhausen's documentary hypothesis theory of the Pentateuch, Deutero-Isaiah, Biblical criticism, and Bultmann's de-mythologizing of the New Testament. As I entered the world of Biblical scholarship, I often felt as though I were wading through a swamp full of dangerous and vicious reptiles. Today, I am no longer innocent or unaware of these radical critiques of the Scriptures. However, as I have continued to read and teach the Bible on a regular basis, my faith in its authenticity as the Word of God has only grown stronger. (It has withstood the most withering attacks from the most brilliant of people.) I still continue to read it every day because my old traveling companion, hope, was with me all the time, fighting whatever damage was done to my belief system.

Hope also restores a sense of wonder, which is so vital to the defeat of sloth. Most normal children in normal situations rarely get depressed. They don't have time, because everything is so new to them. So much to discover, so much to learn. Tragically, as we mature, we lose that sense of wonder somewhere along the way. Life becomes dull, commonplace. "Been there, done that" is the motto of an apathetic, slothful generation.

Hope rejuvenates our sense of discovery, like my friend who learned to swim with the dolphins. It humbles our pride with a vision of the grandeur of God. How little we truly know about this earth. How much more there is left to discover! Hope pulls us forward with a mounting sense of adventure, even turning dread death into a mere passageway to a better, more exciting life.

"GOD IS YOUNGER THAN ALL ELSE..."

"Youth is a cause for hope," wrote Aquinas. "For youth, the future is long and the past is short."[9] Who has not held a baby in one's arms and dreamed of what this little one could become? Everything is possible, no hope too outlandish. Then life catches up with us as we age. With each decision we make, with every year that passes, our options begin to narrow. Soon we reach a point where our past is longer than our future on this earth. We face our mortality, foreshadowed by the growing weakness of our bodies, and hope begins to fade as well. Such is the destiny for all secular hope, whether it be placed in the idea of human progress or a socialist worker's paradise or even the selfish ambitions of individuals.

Supernatural hope, our second theological virtue, is just the opposite, for, as Josef Pieper says, "it is actually rooted in a much more substantial youthfulness. It bestows on mankind a 'not yet' that is entirely superior to and distinct from the failing strength of man's natural hope. Hence it gives man such a 'long' future that the past seems 'short,' however long and rich his life."[10]

Hope restores our childlike faith, and I am firmly convinced that we shall spend all eternity as youthful beings at the height of our physical and intellectual energy, bursting with new ideas and great projects for the future. We shall laugh and play and work with complete abandon as we are led by God himself who is, as St. Augustine wryly observed, "younger than all else."[11]

HOPE IN GOD

Hope teaches us to believe again in miracles. To be told by a doctor that, "It's in God's hands now," is not some new piece of information -- it was always thus. Such confidence is what gave the early Christians the ability to sing as they were led to the Roman Coliseum to be torn to shreds by wild animals. It was the motivation behind Queen Esther's words as she prepared to face the King and a possible death sentence: "If I perish, I perish." Examples such as this could be multiplied by the thousands, yet, in every case, they were not concerned about the outcome, for their hope was in God, not in the outcome. To be delivered from death is wonderful, to die and be with God -- far better. How petty of Solomon to worry about his legacy! How utterly boring and meaningless it is to view life from a human perspective. He should have listened to his father, who wrote:

Why are you downcast, O my soul?
Why so disturbed within me?
Put your hope in God, for I will yet
praise him, my Savior and my God.[12]

Part Five

GLUTTONY

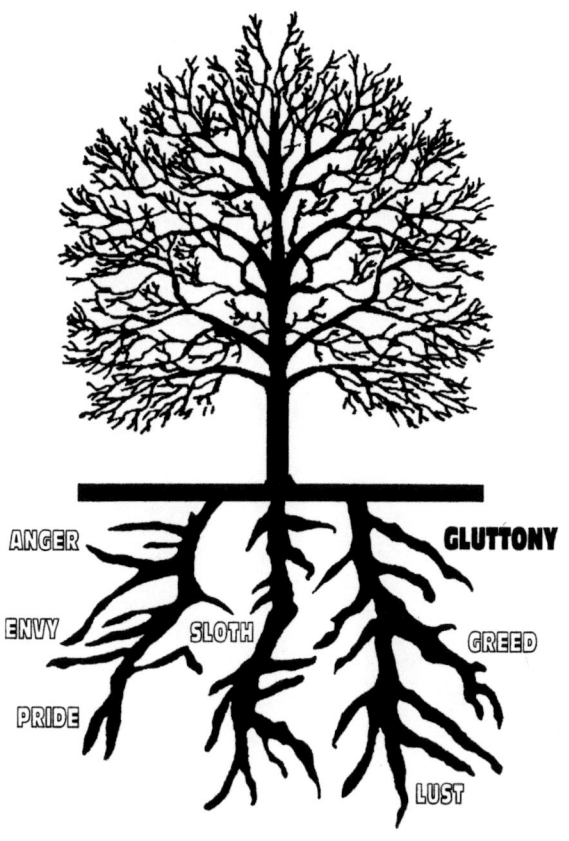

GLUTTONY: An insatiable desire for food, drink or drugs caused by an emptiness of the soul, blinding us to the consequences of our actions.

THE LOVE OF SELF: Awakens within us a sense of danger as we experience how costly and precious we are to God.

HE DIED A SLAVE

The two hunters paused on the top of the ridge to catch their breath. Below them, stretched as far as they could see, campfires flickered in the growing dusk like stars in the heavens. For a few moments they sat silently, watching the peaceful scene with a growing unease.

"What are we going to say to them?" asked Labish, rising quickly from his perch.

"We will tell them the truth," replied Reuben, "that there is not a single deer or wild hog within a hundred miles of this place. Only this scrawny rabbit." As he spoke, he slowly pulled their only prize out of his bag.

"What good will that thing do anyone? There's hardly enough meat there for the two of us."

"Exactly what I was thinking," said Reuben with a twinkle in his eye. "After all, Moses taught us not to muzzle the ox!"

They both laughed. Labish began building a fire, while Reuben quickly dressed the rabbit and placed in on a spit.

The smell of the cooking meat was almost unbearable for the two men. They sat turning the rabbit carefully over the fire as if it were made of gold. Finally, when it was done, they attacked it ravenously with their hunting knives.

Labish howled, "Oh, this is the first taste of meat I've had in months."

Reuben said nothing, preferring not to waste one moment on idle chatter.

When they were down to gnawing on the bones, Reuben spoke, "What a sight we are. Why, back in Egypt, I wouldn't have given this stringy meat to my dog! Sometimes I wonder if Moses knows what he is doing."

"Egypt was not that great," replied Labish, absent-mindedly scratching the scars on his shoulder.

"You forget, my friend, that I was an assistant to one of the overseers. Every evening, we had leeks, onions, garlic and as much fish as we liked. My Sara could make the best lamb

73

stew you have ever tasted! But, now, all we have is this manna!"

"Don't mention that word to me," complained Labish. "Sometimes I think I will vomit if I have to eat that again."

"What are we doing in this God-forsaken desert? I, for one, am ready to go back home, like Shaphat and his clan. He was always a smart cookie. You know, he asked me to go back with him."

"Well, it's a good thing you didn't. I heard last week that some Bedouins found them about three weeks journey from here. All thirty were dead!"

"Really!" Reuben said with alarm, "I hadn't heard that -- what happened to them?"

"Ran out of food and water. It seems that the manna only appears near our main camp. They just had enough provisions for a few days, because they were counting on the manna to get them back to Egypt."

The seriousness of their plight silenced the two men. Both felt a chill as the cool night wind fanned their fire.

"This is all Moses' fault!" Reuben blurted out with a vehemence that surprised Labish. "We were all better off in Egypt."

"Speak for yourself," said Labish. "As much as I hate it, this manna is still a blessing from God. I would rather eat it the rest of my life than go back to slavery."

"Slavery!" Reuben snorted, "We have simply traded one master for another. Instead of the Egyptian task masters, we now have the law and this tyrant Moses."

"No," argued Labish, "Moses has taught us that everyone is under the law, even him. You can't compare our bondage in Egypt with our present situation. If I am going to die, I want to die as a free man, not as a slave."

"You may get your wish sooner than you think, my friend. Let's get some sleep. Tomorrow will not be a good day."

The next morning, the two men headed down the mountain into camp. There was nothing else to do but to

74

announce their gloomy report: No wild game to be found anywhere.

As the news began to circulate among the people, riots broke out. Fighting and wailing and cursing, their anger soon turned on Moses. "Were there no graves in Egypt that you brought us out to this wilderness to die? We remember the fish we ate and the leeks and garlic; now we see nothing but this manna!"

Moses quickly removed himself from the rabble, telling them that he would seek the voice of God. That evening, he announced the results: "Get ready, for tomorrow you will all eat meat. Not just for one day, or two or ten or twenty days, but for a whole month -- until it comes out of your nostrils and you loathe it!"

The people stared at him in disbelief. There were over six hundred thousand men plus as many women and children. Where was this meat to come from? Moses had no answer.

Later that night, a wind went out from the Lord and drove quail in from the sea. It brought them down all around the camp three feet thick as far as a day's walk in any direction!

Reuben was jubilant as everyone made a mad dash to begin preparing the precious food. Labish, however, was more circumspect, sensing that this miracle contained both a blessing and a curse. He decided to only eat manna that evening.

People were dancing and laughing as the smell of roasted quail filled the air. As they sat down to eat, even while the meat was still between their teeth, the anger of the Lord burned against the people and many were struck dead from a severe plague. Reuben was one of those.

The next day, Labish volunteered to bury his old hunting partner. The place was named Kibroth Hattaavah or "the graves of craving" by the people. Labish thought another name might be just as fitting, and so wrote sadly on Reuben's tombstone, "He died a slave."

THE SEDUCTIVE SIRENS OF GLUTTONY

First thou shalt arrive where the enchanter Sirens dwell,
they who seduce men. The imprudent man
who draws near them never returns,
for the Sirens, lying in the flower-strewn fields,
will charm him with sweet song;
but around them the bodies of their victims lie in heaps.
The Odyssey, Book XII

In Greek mythology, there existed an island off the coast of Sicily that was populated by woman-like beings known as Sirens. In some accounts, they are depicted as half-woman, half-bird creatures whose songs were so beautiful that they lured many sailors to their deaths.

Ulysses, the Greek hero who was returning home from Troy, was warned beforehand of the irresistible charm of the Sirens' song. Thus, he took proper precautions. Since he wished to hear them, he stuffed his men's ears with wax and had himself lashed to the main mast of his ship. He gave explicit orders that they were not to loose him no matter what he said. Sure enough, as they drew near the island, the music was so captivating and so enticing that Ulysses alternately begged and ordered to be released, but to no avail. Instead, he was saved by the earlier warning he had received. It was said by the ancient Greeks that he was the only man ever to have survived the fatal music of the Sirens.

GRAVES OF CRAVING

Whether they appear as mythological Sirens or mermaids or, as in our Biblical story, very real quail from heaven, the message is the same: Beware the seductive delights in life, for they stand at the gates to destruction. Failure to recognize this was Reuben's mistake in the previous story. Pleasure can lead to the "graves of craving."

76

Eating and drinking are the two most fundamental pleasures of life. Used properly, these simple joys can encourage the disheartened, renew the weak and comfort the fearful. In addition to that, the celebration of food plays a central role in the Bible, from the Old Testament feasts, to Holy Communion, to the future marriage supper of the Lamb. Feasting and celebration are just as much a part of the Christian life as fasting. Therefore, a hearty enjoyment of food does not constitute the sin of gluttony, nor is obesity always a telltale sign. Rather, it is a spiritual problem in which a person's relationship with food and drink have become inverted. The master has become the servant. Therein lies the difficulty.

> # Beware the seductive delights in life, for they stand at the gates to destruction.

When we give ourselves over to gluttony, a special kind of blindness sets in. Whereas pride, envy and anger blind us to our responsibility for the problem, gluttony, greed and lust prevent us from seeing the consequences of our actions.

How many social drinkers ever thought they would end up as alcoholics? How many smokers believed they would die of cancer? These are things that happen to other people, not to me! The pleasures of life have a way of leading us slowly down the path of destruction, whispering in our ear that all is well, blinding us with beautiful scenery and beautiful people until it is too late. In the sin of gluttony, we literally dig our graves with our teeth.

THE TEST OF MONOTONY

Our story is an adaptation of that which is found in Numbers 11. Here, the Israelites are in the second phase of their journey, which began in Egypt and culminated in the conquest of the Promised Land. Now they are in the merciless desert with nothing to eat but manna. They complain to Moses that back in Egypt they had fish and melons, garlic and leeks. They had become sick of manna. I can certainly sympathize with their plight.

A number of years of ago, my wife and I worked and lived at a Christian mission based in Europe. As with other such ministries, the large number of people living together in one place made food a special challenge. Meals tended to follow a predictable routine. Every day for lunch we always had the same thing: soup and sandwiches. Often the soup was a carryover from the day before, with new ingredients added. Not a few jokes were made about the mystery soup!

There were times when it got a little boring, but most of us adjusted without too many problems. I will never forget, however, one woman from California who had a hard time with our rather monotonous diet. Part of her problem was that she worked in the kitchen and had to stir the same pot of soup day after day. As the days went by, this somewhat "high strung" lady's complaints became louder, until one day she just "snapped." While we were all having lunch at the table, she suddenly ran out of the room, yelling, "I can't take it anymore!" and henceforth refused to eat lunch with the rest of us.

This was the stage the people had reached when Reuben and Labish returned from their unsuccessful hunt. The complaining had begun to build, until it reached a crescendo of riots and a final confrontation with Moses. They were at a breaking point, and something had to be done.

I have often wondered why God allowed this to happen as he did. Why did he give them manna, which, though sweet to the taste, became monotonous and boring after a while? Was he merely being cruel and sadistic? I don't think so. In fact, the Bible tells us the reason in Deuteronomy 8:2-3:

Remember how the Lord your God led you all the way in the desert these forty years, to humble you and to test you in order to know what was in your heart, whether or not you would keep his commandments. He humbled you, causing you to hunger and then feeding you with manna, which neither you nor your fathers had known,

*to teach you that man does not live on bread alone but
on every word that comes from the mouth of the Lord.*

Gluttony is a misplaced dependency. Like the mythological Sirens, it lulls us into a trance, making us think we must have the desired object at any cost. Heedless of the consequences, we rush in, gorging our bodies with food, alcohol or drugs. They become our master and we, their pitiful slaves. Adam and Eve discovered this too late as they ate from the tree of the knowledge of good and evil. Israel experienced this in her lust for meat. As Moses wrote the above verses, he must have thought back to the "graves of craving" and the hard lesson learned there. He prayed that his people might understand the profound truth that "man does not live by bread alone but on every word that comes from the mouth of the Lord."

**Gluttony lulls us into a trance,
making us think we must have
the desired object at any cost.
Then food, alcohol or drugs
become our master,
and we, their pitiful slaves.**

Sadly, they did not. Over and over again, the pleasures of life produced amnesia about God. As they grew rich, so did their appetites. More luxury, more delicate wines -- more, more, more! John Calvin once wrote:

*When God pours forth what is needful with a liberal
hand, he tests our temperance to see whether we will
use these gifts with frugality and gratitude. To restrain
ourselves in the midst of abundance is a virtue
well-pleasing to God, and reveals a grateful heart."*

The central challenge of gluttony is how well we handle pleasure. Do we overindulge or do we show restraint? The answer to that question will be determined by the third and greatest of the theological virtues: love.

THE HOLY GRAIL OF MODERN MAN

As we stand at on the threshhold of the third millennium, our society seems to be ensnared in a truly wicked paradox. Never before in the history of mankind have so many books been published about the need for us to love ourselves. Yet, at the same time, never before has there been such an epidemic of low self-esteem.

Today, there is a kind of desperate search in our culture for ways to shore up the sagging image of ourselves, spanning the gamut from breast implants to designer clothing. Just as medieval knights embarked on fruitless quests to find the holy grail, so does modern man seek frantically for the blessings of self-esteem and dignity.

I am reminded of C.S. Lewis' statement in <u>The Abolition of Man</u>:

> *In a sort of ghastly simplicity we remove the organ and demand the function. We make men without chests* (men without morality) *and expect of them virtue and enterprise. We laugh at honour and are shocked to find traitors in our midst.*[1]

This is precisely the problem that secular culture has created for itself. It tells people that they are nothing more than highly developed animals. It gives mothers the right to kill their unborn children and contemplates euthanasia of the elderly or terminally ill. It glorifies sex without commitment, commercializes every human relationship, and then tells us to feel good about ourselves! It is a conundrum from which society can never escape. While the motivation behind it may be freedom from religious scruples, the actual consequence is greater bondage to gluttony (the addictive society), leading to despair and self-loathing. Man without God is not free. He is adrift on a sea of sinfulness, drawing ever closer to the jagged rocks of the Sirens' island.

> Man without God is not free.
> He is adrift on a sea of sinfulness,
> drawing ever closer
> to the jagged rocks of the Sirens' island.

The problem, of course, is that modern man is looking in all the wrong places. Our true sense of worth and value comes only from a relationship with God. It is only in him and in his Word that we discover our true selves. Any attempt to build a philosophy of human dignity apart from God is doomed to fail, for only he is the one who could say to Moses, "I am who I am." He is self-existent, we are contingent; he is the premise, we are the conclusion.

The battle for abortion will never be won or lost in the courtroom or in politics. It did not begin in 1973, nor will it end anytime soon. In this struggle, the Supreme Court is entirely irrelevant. Abortion is simply the consequence of a pagan understanding of man which completely strips him of all dignity and value. Only in the Scriptures do we find that man is created in the image of God. Only here do we read of his fall into sin and God's valiant quest to redeem him. We are loved, we are cherished by God himself! We bear his image! This is our foundation for self-esteem, and this alone.

THE LOVE OF SELF

One of the common statements made by ex-drug addicts and alcoholics is that they engaged in such behavior in order to fill an "emptiness" inside. They hungered for a connection or union with something or someone and settled instead for destructive substitutes. In so many of these cases, only a spiritual experience with God was able to break the power of their addiction.

81

The original vacuum experienced by these people was not low self-esteem, as our society would have it, but rather a spiritual void. More specifically, it was a yearning for love which brings union between individuals, as well as within the individual himself. A man who hates himself is a man divided.

From a Biblical point of view, it is natural for people to love themselves. The second greatest commandment, according to Jesus, is to "love your neighbor *as you love yourself.*" (Emphasis mine.) Thus, not only is love of self taken for granted, it even becomes the model or standard of love for others. However, every time we sin, we experience shame and guilt, which in turn destroy some of our self-esteem. In the diagram below, two paths are depicted. On the left, the wrong use of pleasure pulls us down into sin, shame, and consequently, loss of self-esteem. On the right is the only way to restore what sin has damaged. Through repentance and confession of sin we begin to regain our self-control. Only then will a person experience a healthy self-esteem. There are no shortcuts.

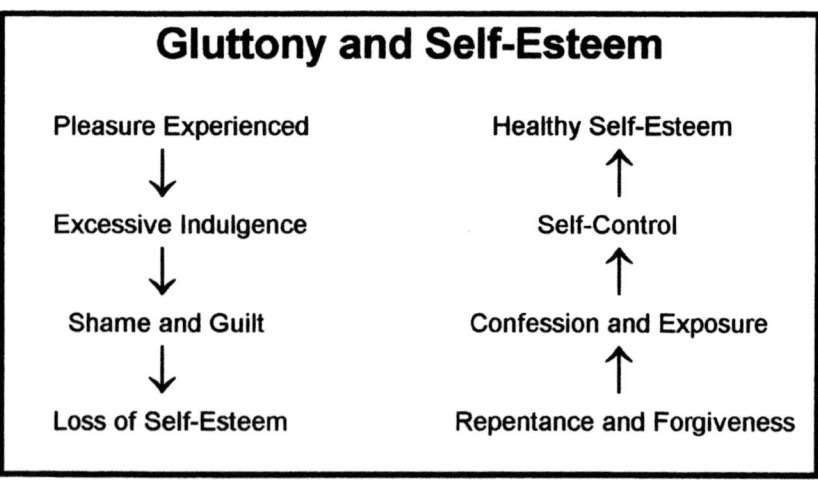

A well-fed man does not steal a loaf of bread. A person with purpose does not commit suicide, nor does a happy husband seek after extra-marital affairs. In the same way, as we stay close to the Lord, his love so fills us that the temptations of illicit pleasures lose their charm.

82

Aye, there's the rub. Anyone who has been a Christian for longer than six months to a year knows the waning and waxing of spiritual desire. It is not long before the deadly enemy of sloth creeps in and begins to dampen our enthusiasm for Bible study and worship.

If we give in to our sloth, the temptations of food, drink and sex (the most basic pleasures of life) begin to gain a foothold. The fact that all three of these are connected should not surprise us. Even the word "orgy" itself was originally used to describe the wild parties devoted to the god Dionysius which involved frenzied eating, drinking and sexual activity.

Such behavior, however, creates guilt and shame. These, in turn, destroy self-esteem. Thus, we should see low self-esteem as the *result* of sinful behavior, not the *cause*. Famed psychiatrist Gerald May agrees:

Most [addicts] *seemed to have led relatively normal lives before the addiction started. They had been capable of authentic respect for themselves, and in their dealings with others they had demonstrated compassion, honesty, and straightforwardness. I had to conclude that the symptoms of addictive personality were caused by the addiction, not the cause of it.* [2]

As usual, the world has got it wrong. Since they refuse to admit they are sinners, the only other way to build self-esteem is through daily affirmations, removal of competition in which failure might result, and a host of other familiar tactics.

Jesus profoundly understood the needs of people trapped by gluttony. Have you ever considered the different ways he acted toward the religious leaders on the one hand and the publicans and "sinners" on the other? This can be seen more clearly if we follow this traditional division between the "respectable" sins of pride, envy and anger (which call out the Pharisee in us) and the more "shameful" sins of gluttony, greed and lust. The prostitutes, tax collectors and drunkards of Jesus' day did not have to be told they were bad people. They knew it already. Most of them felt condemned in their hearts and ashamed of what they had become. They had sold their birthright as human beings for a cheap thrill or dishonest buck. When they had an encounter with Jesus, he didn't call them whited sepulchers; he didn't make a whip and drive them out of the temple (as if they would be there anyway). Instead, he listened to them, he had dinner with them and, most shockingly, he became their friend. The prophet Isaiah said of him: *"A bruised reed he will not break, and a smoldering wick he will not snuff out."* [3]

He knew that their greatest need was to have restored to their thinking the fact that they are men and women created in the image of God. His love for them inspired a love for themselves.

Part Six

GREED

ANGER

GLUTTONY

ENVY

SLOTH

GREED

PRIDE

LUST

GREED: Elevation of material things above God and others, making money our master.

THE LOVE OF GOD: Creates a deep sense of gratitude for God's overwhelming forgiveness and acceptance, teaching us the true source of security.

THE MISER BECOMES A TRAITOR

Martha gazed at her checklist. So much to do in preparation for the Passover and only six days left! How was she ever going to do it all, especially now that the Master was coming for dinner? She furrowed her brow and returned to her cleaning.

Mary appeared at the back door with Lazarus, carrying a basket of fresh fish. As the two entered the kitchen, Martha exclaimed, "Don't come in here with those things! We will clean them outside. I don't want scales and fish heads in this kitchen."

The two dutifully obeyed their older sister and placed the basket outside. "Martha," ventured Mary, "I have been thinking this morning about what we should do for the Master. He is coming an awfully long way to be with us tonight, and we should have some gift to present to him."

"I have noticed," replied Martha, "that his sandals are looking a bit worn lately. What about getting him a new pair?"

"That's not a bad idea, but I wanted to give him more. After all he has done for us, a pair of sandals would almost be an insult."

"Well, you know he doesn't want anything. Do you remember when that rich landowner tried to give him ten pounds of gold?"

"Yes," laughed Lazarus. "He thought he could buy influence with the Master. Was he ever surprised! All he got was a strong rebuke. I can still remember the look on his face."

The two sisters laughed as their brother imitated the landowner's amazed shock. It was so good to have Lazarus back with them. It seemed like a lifetime ago when he had become sick. Mary remembered the long days of fever, followed by endless coughing, and finally, death. Only a few months ago, her brother, this man making jokes, was buried in a tomb! Who would have ever thought that Jesus could bring a man back from death!

Lazarus was so uncomfortable with his sudden celebrity status that he had become a virtual recluse. Tonight, however, he would sit publicly with Jesus at the table. "No," Mary thought. "After all that Jesus has done for us, a pair of sandals is just not right."

Suddenly, Mary spoke up. "What about the nard?"

The three siblings looked at each other to see if there was any hint of hesitation. This nard represented more than a year's salary. It was part of their inheritance and security for old age. The three of them had agreed long ago that it would never be used or traded without unanimous consent.

Martha responded first. "You're absolutely right, Mary. The perfume would be the best gift we could give him."

Lazarus nodded his head in agreement. "That's a fine idea, but I am afraid he wouldn't accept it, if we just presented him with the jar. That would just be like giving him money, and you know he doesn't care about that. Besides, it should be something more meaningful."

There was silence for several minutes as each of them considered the best way to approach Jesus with such an expensive gift. Suddenly Mary snapped her fingers. "I know the perfect thing. Just leave it to me."

That evening, the house was packed with guests. People were even standing outside in order to get a glimpse of Jesus, as well as of Lazarus, the man brought back from the dead. At a certain time, Mary looked at her brother and sister, and they both nodded knowingly. She took the pint of pure nard and stood before Jesus. The room grew quiet with an air of expectancy. Slowly, she knelt down and unbuckled his sandals. She took the perfume and began to pour it on his feet, carefully wiping them with her hair. The whole room was filled with an indescribable fragrance. Martha and Lazarus looked on proudly, feeling that this had been the perfect way to express their appreciation to the Master.

Abruptly, that precious moment of silence and awe was broken by a nasal voice. "What a waste," Judas whined, "this perfume could have been sold and the money given to the poor!"

Martha's eyes flashed with anger. Who did he think he was, telling them what to do with their own money! She never did like Judas; she didn't trust him. Martha opened her mouth to defend her sister's action, but Jesus spoke first.

"Leave her alone," he said to Judas. "It was intended that she should use this perfume for the day of my burial. You will always have the poor among you, but you will not always have me."

After the meal that evening, Judas went for a walk by himself. He was embarrassed and angry at what had taken place. "It seems as though I am the only practical person around here," he grumbled. "I can understand that empty-headed Mary doing something like that, although you would think Martha would have better sense. But, Jesus!--" he stopped suddenly. "I thought I knew him; I thought we agreed on the fundamentals. He really disappointed me tonight. I expected him to stop her from such waste." As treasurer of the group, he felt he should be consulted on all financial decisions. Though he would never admit it, however, much of the money designated for the poor ended up in his own hidden "nest egg." "After all," he thought wryly, "Who's poorer than me?"

He felt a pain in his chest as he calculated the expense of the nard. He continued walking like a man with business on his mind. When he came to a certain house, he glanced furtively behind and quickly opened the door.

"Did anyone follow you?" the man asked anxiously.

"Of course not," replied Judas. "They are all too busy throwing good money down the drain."

"I take it, from the sound of your voice, that we have a deal?" He reached out to Judas as he spoke.

"Yes," answered Judas. "Give me thirty pieces of silver, and I will personally hand him over to you."

"Agreed," the other man chuckled.

THE GLITTERING MIRAGE OF GREED

The Fata Morgana is the most famous mirage in the world. It can be seen over the Strait of Messina between Italy and Sicily, taking the form of fantastic and weird castles rising out of the sea. It is so named for Morgan le Fay, the Arthurian sorceress. As one ventures into the Strait, the cliffs and houses on the opposite shore seem to change shape at will, forming in one moment ordinary houses and in the next, the turreted castles of the enchantress. All of this is accomplished through the distortion and magnification of changing layers of air.

Even a simple mirage like a pool of water in the distance on a hot day can seem so real. But as we draw near, it suddenly vanishes, leaving the promise of cool water or beautiful castles unfulfilled. This is exactly how greed operates. It is a vice that urges us continually in pursuit without ever tasting any satisfaction. Mistaking money for security, we grasp at every nickel and dime, hoping to build a wall of protection against the vicissitudes of life. Only too late do we learn that a slight tremble in the earth's surface, a flash flood from the mountains, or an accidental spark from old wiring can wipe out a lifetime of work in a moment, leaving us with nothing.

Jesus said:

Look at the birds of the air; they do not sow or reap or store away in barns, and yet your heavenly Father feeds them. Are you not much more valuable than they? Who of you by worrying can add a single hour to his life? And why do you worry about clothes? See how the lilies of the field grow. They do not labor or spin. Yet, I tell you that not even Solomon in all his splendor was dressed like one of these. If that is how God clothes the grass of the field, which is here today and tomorrow is thrown into the fire, will he not much more clothe you, O you of little faith?[1]

How different the easy, lighthearted manner of Jesus contrasts with the cold, calculated actions of Judas! One believed his heavenly Father would tend to his needs, while the other fearfully hedged his bets.

THE FEARFUL MISER

The word "miser" comes from Latin and originally meant a wretched or unfortunate person. In modern English it has come to connote a person who deprives himself of all but the bare essentials in order to accumulate money. The adjective "miserable" comes from the same Latin root, which refers to a person who is unhappy, uncomfortable or stingy.

Fear is one of the main reasons for a greedy man's misery. He is terrified by parties or any extravagance lest something be wasted. He vigilantly guards against being cheated and is forever suspicious of the motivations of others. His greatest fear, of course, is that he will lose his money, and he thus goes to great lengths to protect his investments.

Michael P. Green tells this story:

Hetty Green was possibly America's greatest miser. She died in 1915, leaving an estate valued at over one million dollars, but always ate cold oatmeal because it cost too much to heat it. Her son had to suffer through a leg amputation unnecessarily because Hetty wasted so much time looking for a free clinic that he wasn't examined early enough.

Hetty Green was wealthy, but she chose to live like a pauper. Eccentric? Yes. Crazy? Perhaps, but nobody could prove it. She was so foolish that she hastened her own death when she suffered a stroke by becoming too excited over a discussion about the value of drinking skimmed milk.[2]

In contrast to that, one of the most moving scenes in any movie I have ever watched is the last few minutes of the Frank Capra film, "It's A Wonderful Life." George, played by Jimmy

Stewart, deep in debt and bankrupt, yet happy to be alive, rushes home to find his family. As he passes the office of his nemesis, Mr. Potter, he shouts out, "Merry Christmas, Mr. Potter!" The greedy miser retorts, "Go home! The bank examiners and police are waiting for you!" George arrives at his house, pushing past the officers and throwing his arms around his wife and children. Then something wonderful happens. Friends and neighbors, who had heard he was in trouble, show up with a generous outpouring of love and affection. Their monetary gifts more than make up the needed cash, while the angel reminds George, by way of an inscription in a book, that "no man is a failure who has friends."

> ## The extravagance of love is the only real solution to the pettiness of greed.

What a difference there was between the loneliness and isolation of Mr. Potter, the miserly businessman, and the warmth and security of love in George's home! Surely, the extravagance of love is the only real solution to the pettiness of greed. If only Judas could have understood the devotion behind that gift of nard, he never would have interrupted such a sacred moment. Every time we give freely from a heart overflowing with gratitude, without strings attached, we lessen the power of greed in our lives. We remind ourselves that we are the master and money is our servant, not the other way around.

THE RECKLESS PRODIGAL

The opposite of the careful miser is the reckless prodigal.[3] After demanding his share of the inheritance, he goes to live in a far away country where he spends everything he has. The only job he can find is caring for pigs, an abomination to the Jews of Jesus' day. His careless lifestyle has reduced him to the lowest possible state.

On one hand, the prodigal's greed seems closer to that of gluttony, while the miser's resembles aspects of envy. They only have two things in common: Both have failed in their management or stewardship of money, and both refuse to give. The prodigal's generosity at throwing parties and treating his friends to a great time should not be confused with true, unselfish giving. We seem to have forgotten in modern times that simple, indiscriminate largess accomplishes nothing but the dwindling of one's fortunes. Rather, it is the giving of oneself that is important.

The test to determine if one's giving is wasteful or helpful can best be measured in the effect it has on the recipients. When the prodigal's money ran out, so did his friends! They knew he was not interested in them as people. Rather, they were witnesses to his hedonism, hirelings for a night's pleasure. No love or bond of gratitude was created, and when hard times came, no warm circle of friends gathered round to help. In the final analysis, both the miser and the prodigal go home alone, condemned to the isolation of greed.

THE RICH FOOL

Jesus told one other story which, along with the miser and the prodigal, forms a fitting trilogy for our discussion of this subject. It is known as the Parable of the Rich Fool.[4] It's a story about a good, hard-working farmer who began to prosper. Therefore, he started making plans for the future, such as tearing down his barns and building bigger ones. He also began to anticipate the day he could retire, take life easy and "eat, drink and be merry." But God said to him, "You fool! This very night your life will be demanded from you. Then who will get what you have prepared for yourself?"

"This," says Jesus, "is how it will be with anyone who stores up things for himself but is not rich toward God." When I have taught on this parable in the past, I have seen some people bristle and become indignant. "What possible sin did this farmer commit?" they ask. "He is only being a good businessman.

Certainly you're not saying we shouldn't save for retirement or plan for the future?"

No, that's not the point of this story. The point is that we must be very careful not to allow the "deceitfulness of riches" to lull us to sleep. As stated at the beginning of this chapter, money has a way of making us feel secure. We think, "if only we had a little more, everything would be all right." All of this is very dangerous, because it hides the hard truth that all worldly security is only a mirage. The richest man or woman in the world will one day die, just like the poorest. Wealth, fame, and popularity are as dependable as the weird castles of the Fata Morgana. They evaporate as quickly as they appear. If that is where your security lies, then indeed, you are a fool.

CONSECRATED AMBITION

Not long ago, a thought-provoking TV special hosted by John Stossel was aired.[5] The subject was greed. Throughout the documentary, the commentator praised the good that greed had done for society. Greed, he said, had made America great, and we should not feel guilty about it nor consider it a sin.

With all due respect to John Stossel (whom I admire), I must disagree. Yes, we can concede that the activities of greedy people may help the overall economy on the large scale. However, such a sin will only destroy those individuals caught in its clutches.

I rather suspect that our disagreement is more about semantics than substance. The good and productive quality that Stossel and others were talking about would have better been described as ambition. The Bible tells us:

Whatever you do, work at it with all your heart, as working for the Lord, not for men, since you know that you will receive an inheritance from the Lord as a reward. It is the Lord Christ you are serving.[6]

In other words, everything we do must be done with excellence. Our work, whether it be manufacturing, selling, teaching, or raising children, demands our whole heart. This requires ambition, which is a positive attribute, contrary to some super-spiritual views, such as: "My real job is witnessing for Jesus; working is just what I do to keep food on the table so I can witness." The Bible never demeans the importance of so-called "secular" work. (After all, Jesus only spent three years preaching, and, we may assume, over twenty years in a carpenter's shop.) If we truly believe that every Christian is a priest before God, then whatever work he or she does is sacred.

It is also wrong to confine the role of businessmen to that of merely financing the work of God. To see them as "cash cows" for the kingdom is not only insulting, but also a fundamental misunderstanding of what work is all about. As businessmen and businesswomen, they are providing jobs for other people, producing products to make life better and contributing to the overall wealth of the nation. These are holy tasks which have an intrinsic value in themselves.

Greed is selfish; Godly ambition is selfless. Greed uses people and exploits them for some ulterior purpose. Godly ambition develops people and helps them to grow to become producers themselves. The Christian entrepreneur may very well be led by God to build a business empire of unparalleled wealth. However, in the process, he will inspire and encourage others, not selfishly use them as stepping stones in his rise to success.

Ambition is a two-edged sword which can either create a great man or woman who is loved by later generations, or produce an evil genius who joins the ranks of the dictators and robber barons of the past. The difference will depend upon the love of God in the heart.

THE LOVE OF GOD

Faith and hope are so intimately linked together that it is impossible to conceive of one without the other. We are told in Romans 10:17 that faith is inspired or originated in our hearts by hearing the Word of God. I think the same is true with hope as well. These two "theological virtues" are birthed in our hearts and made strong as we hear and read God's Word.

Love is different, however. Love is inspired by love. Love is created by love. We learn to love by the love we received as children. In a relationship between a man and woman, the love of one inspires a reciprocal love in the other.

So it is with God. "We love because he first loved us."[7] This is such a key thought because it tells us that the initiative all along has been with him. Like the son of a wealthy father, God puts his arm around us and shows us the wonders of the universe. Since it all belongs to him, it all belongs to us to enjoy and to use as well.

How must the Father laugh at us as we grasp greedily and hoard everything our puny hands can reach! He understands our insecurities and lavishes more love upon us. Consider Jesus at Zacchaeus' home. Here is a man who has become wealthy by exploiting his position as a tax collector. Instead of a lecture, however, Jesus invites himself over for dinner. What an act of love for one who does not deserve it! As love begets love, Zaccheus stands and announces that those he cheated will be repaid fourfold, and half of his wealth given to the poor. The fear of the miser is exorcised by the love of God.

> # God's love turns money into a servant.

The prodigal returns, ashamed and embarrassed at his own foolish choices, certain that never again will he enjoy his position as an honored son. His head droops down so that he cannot see a figure in the distance, running toward him with outstretched arms. Soon, however, he hears the footsteps and lifts his gaze to see his father. As he collapses into his father's arms, he hears the sweetest words ever spoken: "My son has returned!" His wastefulness is healed by the gratitude of love's second chance.

As they lay the rich fool in his coffin, his hands are empty. He never understood that his houses and lands and barns and even he, himself -- all belonged to God. His life was so full of things that there was no room left for the Father's love. What a tragedy!

"No man can serve two masters. Either he will hate the one and love the other, or he will be devoted to the one and despise the other. You cannot serve both God and Money."[8] God's love turns money into a servant.

Part Seven

LUST

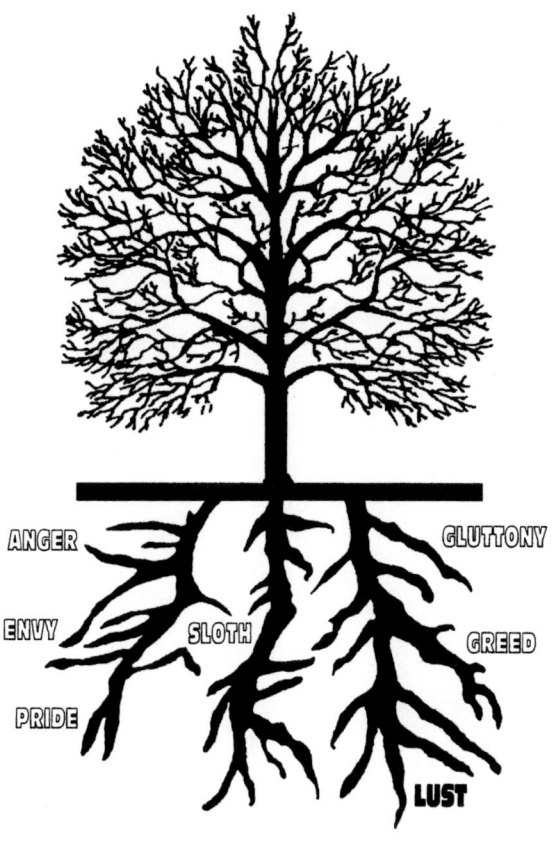

LUST: Public exposure and degradation of sex, a sacred gift from God, resulting in shame and loss of true intimacy with God and others.

THE LOVE OF OTHERS: Restores our humanity and dignity by calling us to a life of self-sacrifice rather than self-gratification.

HOW THE MIGHTY HAVE FALLEN

Ah, springtime in Jerusalem! The shepherds begin their annual preparations for the summer trek to the highlands. It is a time for weddings, a time to plow and plant the crops for another year.

Many lambs will be born in anticipation of the most solemn and yet joyous festival of the year -- Passover! His mouth watered as the memories flooded his mind. Every year, it became more meaningful to remember the Exodus and the Red Sea and Moses, the great judge.

Now he was a judge. For two decades he had assumed Moses' mantle, and what a heavy mantle it was. So, maybe he did stray a few times -- well, maybe *many* times -- but what difference does that make? Look at all the good he had done for his country; look at the enemies who now respected them.

Yes, there had been many women, yet none so beautiful as she. He remembered the first night they had met and the many enjoyable evenings lasting into the wee hours of the morning. He knew it was wrong; yet, if people only understood the responsibilities and temptations of his position, they would be less critical.

Suddenly, he felt a sharp pain in his side, then another. He heard voices in the darkness, vicious and cruel. Instinctively, he opened his eyes but saw nothing. Instantly, he was jarred back from his memories of the past to the present reality. Now there were others kicking him in the side.

"Get up, Hebrew swine! Today is the great festival, and you're our entertainment."

He quickly rose to his full height and for a moment, the blows stopped as the men backed off. He stood a good two heads taller than the largest man.

They soon secured the ropes and led him into the sunlight. Though his eyes had been gouged out, he could still feel the warmth of the late morning sun. In the distance he could hear the raucous noises of the crowds, mixed with music and the roar of lions.

Regret filled his heart as he submissively followed the direction of the ropes. If only he had stayed away from her. If only he had listened to his parents, none of this would be happening. The mantle of Moses! He didn't deserve it.

Yet, in spite of his feelings of self-loathing, in spite of the emptiness in his soul, he sensed a vague stirring of something from more innocent days. It felt pure and clean for just a moment and then flitted away like a butterfly. It filled him with longing for something he only vaguely remembered -- a sense of purpose, a clearing of the mind.

"Hear O Israel, the Lord our God, the Lord is One!" he uttered loudly and defiantly. Laughter greeted his ears. "So the honorable judge still believes in the Lord? Well? Where is he now? Our gods are greater than him! Long live Dagon! LONG LIVE DAGON!"

Suddenly, the cry which had begun with just a few voices was now echoed by what sounded like thousands. "I must be in the temple arena," he thought to himself. "The entire place must be full."

His tormentors led him to the center where everyone could see. He heard the mocking announcement, "For your amusement, we present the magnificent and powerful Samson." They pulled on the ropes tied to his arms and legs like a marionette, forcing him to dance. The crowd loved it and roared their approval.

Samson, who had once been the champion of his people, was now an object of ridicule, a pathetic clod of humiliation. Young boys surrounded him and lightly stabbed him with their lances. The crowds laughed in delight as the blind man lunged after them in vain.

"Having trouble, big boy?" a feminine voice taunted.

"Delilah, is that you?" In the confusion of the moment, he hadn't heard her chariot approaching.

"What do you think, stupid Hebrew?" She snorted in disgust. "Not so handsome now that your eyes are gone."

Now a chant arose from the throats of the spectators, "De-li-lah! De-li-lah! De-li-lah!" So, what he had heard was true. Since his capture and imprisonment, Delilah had become a kind of national heroine. He chuckled at the thought.

He heard her chariot drive away and, mercifully, the "entertainment" came to a temporary halt. He asked one of the servants who guided him to lead him to the main pillars of the temple.

As he felt the massive structures beneath his hands, an idea began to form in his mind. "Are these two pillars the supports for the entire temple?"

The servant's laughter rang out. "Of course they are. Do you plan to push them over?"

For just a moment, he faltered. What was he doing? God's Spirit had left him long ago. Yet, from somewhere an old, familiar sense of determination began welling up within him. He found himself praying, "O Sovereign Lord, remember me. O God, please strengthen me just once more, and let me with one blow get revenge on the Philistines for my two eyes."

He reached out with both arms and felt the huge stone structures with his hands. He sensed again God's anointing and blessing. He cried out in a loud voice, "Let me die with the Philistines!"

Samson pushed with all his might. He felt the pillars beginning to give way and a noise like none he had ever heard, a crashing, thunderous scraping, followed by cries of alarm and panic. Three thousand men and women perished that day in the temple. Thus, in his death, Samson killed more of his enemies than while he lived.

THE KRYPTONITE OF LUST

Superman, alias Clark Kent, was my hero as a boy. Every month I eagerly anticipated the next issue of Marvel Comics to see what jams the man from Krypton would get into next. The writers and publishers would tease us with headlines such as: "Next Month: Superman Goes Mad," or "The Death of Superman." They knew that this character had a fundamental problem: his invincibility. There was never a question that he would win the next battle. He didn't suffer the existential angst of Batman or the blindness of Daredevil. In every way, he was perfect: a civic-minded, well-balanced, unbeatable hero. That simply would not do! Therefore, in order to build suspense and meaningful conflict, an arch villain had to be created, namely Lex Luthor, who discovered Superman's one weakness -- kryptonite. Exposure to even a small rock from his home planet was like poison to the man of steel.

In the same way, the "superman" of Israel suffered from one fatal weakness -- and it wasn't baldness. Rather, his Achilles heel was lust. In every other way, he appeared to be an excellent, even exceptional leader, until it came to the opposite sex. In Samson's early years, women were playthings or pawns to be used for political intrigue. He seemed to be the classic playboy, moving from one conquest to the next, until he met Delilah.

Normally, when we think of lust, we focus on the way in which it has caused men to abuse and mistreat women. The irony of the Samson story, however, is that now, the victor became the victim. In this Philistine woman, "superman" had met his match.

Conquest, victor, match -- this is the vocabulary of lust. In every human relationship, we are faced with a challenge: Will I use this person for my own selfish pleasure or will I lovingly give of myself for his or her benefit? The roads diverge, and love so often is the one less taken. Love creates a bond between people which protects, nurtures and humanizes. It is the cement which holds families and communities together through the worst of times. Love calls us to lay aside our petty, selfish interests for the good of others. Lust, on the other hand, is a corrosive acid that eats away at the very foundations of all that we hold dear. Like kryptonite, it poisons and weakens our grip on things spiritual. A man who had a problem with pornography once said to me, "It's like having a hole in my bucket. I can feel so close to God and have the best of intentions and then, when I look at porno, it all seems to evaporate."

> # Conquest, victor, match;
> # this is the vocabulary of lust.

Judges 16:4 says: "Some time later, he (Samson) fell in love with a woman in the Valley of Sorek whose name was Delilah." While it seems that Samson did have some true feelings mixed in with his lust for Delilah, there is no hint from the text that she reciprocated them in any way. Rather, she appears as a heartless, conniving woman whose only interest was in capturing the great judge by discovering the secret of his strength. Blindly, like a lamb led to slaughter, he was manipulated and betrayed. For over 3000 years, his example has warned generations of the deadly power of lust.

Sometimes, I grow weary of the world's mockery of Christian attitudes toward sex. We are accused of being Victorian, hypocritical prudes who want to ruin everyone's fun. Society laughs at our attempts to teach abstinence to young people and then, when faced with an explosion of teen pregnancies, begs us to "do *something, anything*" with these kids.

I admit that the church has not always promoted a healthy view of sex. It is true that we have often erred on the side of asceticism. However, there is a good reason for that. Christians understand that sex, like fire, can be very dangerous. Without fire, civilization would not be possible. It heats our homes, cooks our meals, powers our cars and even operates our computers (in the form of electricity). It is a positive, wonderful blessing -- until it gets out of its proper boundaries. When that happens, it becomes one of the most destructive forces on earth.

So it is with sex. When kept within the proper boundaries of marriage, it is a powerful force for good. However, when it "gets out," it can also become the most ruinous force in human society.

In 1934, J. D. Unwin wrote a book titled <u>Sex and Culture</u>. He set out to test the Freudian idea that civilization is a byproduct of repressed sexuality. He studied 86 different societies from every part of the globe. Commenting on Unwin's study, Philip Yancy writes: "His findings startled many scholars -- above all, Unwin himself -- because all 86 demonstrated a direct tie between monogamy and the 'expansive energy' of civilization."[1]

Unwin, who was not a Christian, concluded: "In human records there is no instance of a society retaining its energy after a complete new generation has inherited a tradition which does not insist on pre-nuptial and post-nuptial continence."

Yancey writes, "He found with no exceptions that these societies flourished during eras that valued sexual fidelity. Inevitably, sexual mores would loosen and the societies would subsequently decline, only to rise again when they returned to more rigid sexual standards."[2]

Interesting, isn't it? Kind of like kryptonite, if you ask me. Unrestrained sexual desire, also known as lust, can weaken an entire nation. Let's turn now to two other ways that this deadly sin affects individuals and families.

LUST AND RESPECT

In a powerful book titled <u>An Affair of the Heart</u>, Laurie Hall (not her real name) courageously tells the story of how lust almost destroyed her family. After eighteen years of marriage, she discovered that her husband was addicted to pornography, which led him to promiscuous behavior with prostitutes. The depth of his involvement and addiction was so great that his life began to unravel. He lost his job, his ability to concentrate, and almost his family as well. He and his wife separated, at which time he began to get some help. Fortunately, their family was saved intact, and today seems to be well on the road to recovery.

I was particularly impressed with the way in which his lust affected her. She writes:

> In my own situation, although I was careful with my clothes and figure, I found that my husband was increasingly critical of the way I looked. Even when friends and acquaintances told me I was an attractive woman, I wasn't attractive enough to compete with eternally young, surgically altered models. . . . In the end, he lost all interest in me as a sexual partner. This had a devastating impact on my view of my worth as a woman. It created such despair in me that I began to let my appearance go. *At last, I looked the way his rejection made me feel -- totally unlovely.* Then I received the picture of me in the wedding dress. Shocked at how far I had deteriorated, I promised myself I'd do whatever was necessary to reclaim the girl in the photograph.
>
> Over the years, I've spoken with other women who have had similar experiences. They tried extra hard to be attractive to their husbands; but the year-after-year battering of constant comparisons with other women and the continual attack on their desirability as a sexual partner wounded their spirits to such a point that they gave up and became the exact opposite of the firm, gorgeous, beautifully made-up women their husbands kept trying to force them to become. *Ironic, isn't it, how pornography creates the exact opposite in real life of what it promotes in fantasy life?*[3] (Emphases mine.)

FOOD FOR THOUGHT:
SIN DECEIVES US BY PROMISING ONE THING
AND DELIVERING THE EXACT OPPOSITE

1. **Anger** deceives us into thinking we are in control, when in actual fact, the angrier we grow, the more impotent and ineffective we become. Flailing our arms about like a gorilla, we are seen as an object of amusement and contempt rather than fear.

2. **Envy** desperately wants to be admired, yet it creates a small-minded, petty person who is anything but admirable.

3. **Pride** is the ultimate deception. Like the makers of the Titanic, we arrogantly proclaim to the world our independence and genius, only to be destroyed by a mindless piece of ice.

4. **Sloth** invites us to a soft, comfortable world, lulling us to sleep, while all the time it is secretly fashioning a chamber of horrors from which some never escape.

5. **Gluttony** tantalizes us with sensual delights of the palate which can lead to such addictions that the sinner needs his daily "fix" just to feel normal.

6. **Greed** deludes us into placing all of our trust and confidence in the most unstable, insecure thing of all -- money.

7. **Lust** promises a voluptuous, exciting sex life in which the norm quickly becomes boring, leading to a vicious cycle of depravity, boredom and deeper depravity.

Lust destroys the self-respect of both perpetrator and victim. We have known for a long time now that rape is just as much about power as it is about sex. I heard of one woman who was kidnapped by a rapist and assaulted several times throughout the night. This man had killed his other victims and threatened to do the same to her. She was very smart, though. Every chance she had, she talked about her family to her tormentor. She showed him pictures of her children and husband. She humanized herself in the eyes of the rapist, and thus survived the horrible ordeal. He let her go because she was no longer merely a sex object. She had become a human being to him, with a name and a family and feelings. In some deep recess of any soul that he had left, a spark of compassion and sense of remorse began to take effect.

LOVE FOR OTHERS

Lust thrives in secrecy. Like the vampire Dracula, it spreads its wings when night falls and hastens back to its hiding place at the crack of dawn. Love, on the other hand, desires transparency and insists on honesty in relationships. Thus, we are often pulled between these two competing forces to either hide or reach out with a trusting heart.

Developing honest, open relationships with others is one of the best antidotes for the sin of lust. As we develop friendships where we learn to trust one another, the darkness begins to dissipate.

The first place to begin, of course, is with one's spouse. He or she should be your best friend, your loyal confidant. I've been amazed in my ministry to see so many marriages where this simply is not a reality. Husbands and wives can become guarded and distant from one another, making extra-marital affairs almost inevitable. Why is it so difficult for most of us to reveal our deepest struggles with the one who shares our bed every night? Fear of rejection or loss of respect? Maybe. Perhaps the real culprit, however, is lack of love. As Paul tells us, "Love always protects, always trusts, always hopes, always perseveres."[4]

The second area of intimacy might surprise many, especially men. In order to strengthen the soul against lust, godly, healthy friendships with members of the same sex are a prerequisite. As nature abhors a vacuum, so will lust invade a lonely heart. Men need each other more than they realize.

Counselors who deal with sex addicts always say the same thing to and about their patients: They have a problem with intimacy. As a result of the secrecy and shame, the lustful person always has his guard up, which precludes true intimacy with other people. Often, he is very lonely, because to share what is really in his heart would be too humiliating.

In some ways, the Samson story does not exactly encourage open disclosure. I can imagine some men, after reading it, wagging their finger in the air, saying, "You see? That's what becomes of all this 'openness' stuff. The man was okay as long as he kept his secret. Then he blabbed to his woman and, boom! It was all over!"

> Lust thrives in secrecy. Like the vampire, Dracula,
> it spreads its wings when night falls
> and hastens back to its hiding place
> at the crack of dawn.
> Exposure to the searing light of day
> will drive a stake right through its heart.

No, this is not the lesson we are to derive from this story. Instead, the moral is to choose your confessors carefully. Certainly, there is a risk in revealing one's secrets. People may not understand; they may become embarrassed or use that information against us later.

We all know this and instinctively test the people we "open up" to. We may share a small problem first and see how they respond. If they pass that test, we may go on to the real issue at hand.

Even Samson did this with Delilah. Three times he tested her through disinformation, and she failed every time. If he had just opened his eyes, he would have seen what was coming, but that was precisely the problem. I don't believe the old adage that "love is blind." Lust is really the one with impaired vision. It blinds us to the consequences of our actions.

Delilah, we are told, pouted, "How can you say, 'I love you,' when you won't confide in me? This is the third time you have made a fool of me and haven't told me the secret of your great strength." The Bible adds, "With such nagging she prodded him day after day until he was tired to death."[5] Amazing, isn't it, that 3000 years later, men and women still haven't come up with a better line than: "How can you say you love me?"

The point is that in order to defeat the sin of lust, it must be exposed to the searing light of day. The openness of love, the acceptance of love, and most of all, the trust of love drives a stake right through the heart of lust. It opens the possibility of true intimacy.

THE HUMANIZING POWER OF LOVE

The New Testament introduced a new meaning to a word that was largely ignored in the ancient world, namely, *agape*. While in classical Greek it was a rather colorless term meaning, "to be fond of, treat respectfully, or to welcome," Christians poured into it a new meaning. *Agape* connotes a love that is entirely unselfish, a love that overwhelms the loved one.

Throughout my years of Bible school and seminary, I worked at various jobs to support myself. One of the toughest, when I was 19 years old, was working at a nursing home. I was a nurse's aide, which meant I attended to the most basic needs of the patients. I kept that job for nine months before moving on, and it was quite an education in its own right. During that time, I witnessed one of the most powerful examples of *agape* that I have ever seen.

One of the patients, named Helen, was in the last stages of some degenerative disease. She was completely catatonic and stiff as a board. It took two of us to dress her every morning because her arms and legs simply refused to bend. Yet dress her we did, for every day, like clockwork, her husband, Tom, would come to visit. He would take her wheelchair and move her to a nice, sunny spot, sit next to her and read the newspaper. I often noticed as I walked by that he held her hand. She was completely incapable of any response whatsoever, yet they sat like that for hours. I thought to myself, "This man understood the vows he took, 'in sickness and in health, until death do us part.'" I thought he must have incredible self-discipline to come and visit her like that every day. That's just what a 19-year-old boy, who knows nothing of love, would think. Today, I'm a

41-year-old man who has known the joy of twenty years of marriage to a wonderful woman. I am beginning to understand that Tom did not have to force himself to come to that nursing home every day. Instead, he couldn't help it.

Where I saw a stiff, old woman, he saw his beautiful, laughing bride. He saw the mother of his children, his best friend in all the world. The truth was, it was a joy to just be there and sit next to his beloved. Though her body had become a prison which kept her mute and immobile, I am sure that on some deep level, she knew he was there.

Helen passed away during my tenure at that nursing home. I was one of the aides assigned to prepare her body for the mortician. What I remember most about it was Tom's reaction. He was heartbroken and sobbed quietly into his handkerchief. I never saw him again after that day.

> **Self-sacrifice is an inevitable outgrowth of love, just as selfishness is of lust.**

Before my eyes I had witnessed a powerful demonstration of true love. What a contrast with the sick, superficial, playboy philosophy so prevalent today in our society. It teaches men to treat women like cars: Every few years, trade her in for a newer model! Plastic surgery is an appropriate necessity for such people because their "love" and self-worth is only skin deep. Theirs is a world that has no place for people like Helen and Tom, and here is the reason why: Lust wants to rule, while love wants to serve. Lust is ever vigilant and self-protective, while love comes bounding in where angels fear to tread. Self-sacrifice is an inevitable outgrowth of love, just as selfishness is of lust.

WHAT WOULD JESUS DO?

Throughout most of this book, I have focused on ways that faith, hope and love help us to defeat sin. There is, however, a role that all Christians are called to play as we seek to minister to the world around us. The most obvious place to look for inspiration is at the life of Jesus.

Below is a chart that I hope clarifies the way in which he interacted with different kinds of sinners. I am afraid that today, we in the church often reverse Jesus' method. We often befriend and respect those with the more secret sins of pride, envy and anger, while vilifying those with lust, greed and gluttony. There is only one exception to the chart below, and that is with the money changers in the temple. Obviously, they were motivated by greed, yet they were part of the "religious establishment" and were thus respected in the community. Sloth is not included because it is such an insidious sin that it rarely appears publicly as the others do. Finally, I do believe Jesus loved both groups equally but understood human nature enough to know that they needed different kinds of medicine.

"RESPECTABLE" SINS OF PRIDE	"DISREPUTABLE" SINS OF LUST
1. *Pharisees* (Pride)	1. *Prostitutes* (Lust)
2. *Sadducees* (Envy)	2. *Tax Collectors* (Greed)
3. *Scribes* (Anger)	3. *"Sinners"* (Gluttony)
(This group thought too highly of themselves. Legalistic religion produces arrogant people.)	(This group were definite outcasts. They felt shame and low self-esteem.)
Jesus sternly rebuked these people, hoping to shock them into a realization of their sin.	**Jesus befriended these people, hoping to heal their shame and restore their dignity.**

CONCLUSION

This famous trinity of faith, hope and love is indeed our greatest ally against the forces of evil in this world. As mentioned at the outset, this conflict in the human heart is by far the most decisive battle in history. There awaits for each of us, however, an ending to the story of this life's struggle -- and a true beginning that is beyond our imagination. In the fictional narrative that follows, we discover, as Paul said in I Corinthians, that while all things of this earth pass away, faith, hope and love remain.[6] Particularly, we will see the power of love demonstrated in the final healing of sin.

THE FINAL HEALING

Joe clawed at his front pocket for the nitroglycerin tablets that had been his constant companions for the past three years. He knew this pain in his chest all too well and the sense of doom that came with it. Three heart attacks in three years! Yet, this one was different; he could feel it. Even as he slipped the tablets into his mouth, he knew deep inside that it was futile. His time was up.

Within seconds the pain subsided. He felt himself drifting as if he were falling asleep, yet never had he been so awake and alert. He seemed to hover near the ceiling as he watched the paramedics work feverishly on his lifeless body. Outside, though he saw the flashing lights of the ambulance and one man shouting orders to everyone else, he heard nothing. He slipped father away, watching his house disappeared quickly on a far, distant horizon. He felt his body (if one could call it that) begin to accelerate at an alarming speed.

Soon he was flying like a rocket over the most captivating landscapes: forest covered mountains, ribbon-like waterfalls, and lakes so clear that every inch of the bottoms were visible. But, as he looked closer, he saw movement. Not the kind of practical, purposeful movement on earth in which things go from point A to point B. This was more of a shimmering or sparkling.

"Sparkling," he thought in wonder, "that's what it is, like the stars at night. Everything seems to sparkle here."

He looked ahead and saw a mountaintop approaching. The summit, looming larger and larger, revealed a lone figure standing tall and rooted, as if for centuries. He felt himself slowing. Obviously, this was his destination. As the tall figure came more clearly into view, a feeling of apprehension came over him.

The funeral was held three days later, to give all the relatives a chance to arrive in the small Texas town of Gladewater. Though Joe's death was sudden, it was not unexpected. After all, a man can only take so many heart attacks.

The casket was opened by the request of the family so people could say their final good-byes. The small room was packed with friends and business associates and neighbors. People were even standing outside for their chance to pay their respects.

For most of his life, Joe had been something of a tragic figure, at least professionally. From the time his father died when he was ten, he had developed a fierce, independent spirit. A short stint in the Marines only intensified this aspect of his character. After fulfilling his obligation to his country, Joe went into business for himself. He married his high school sweetheart, Margaret, and together they bought an old, ramshackle farmhouse. They went into the chicken business just as the price for eggs and poultry hit rock bottom. This saddled the young couple with a debt that would last the next twenty years of their marriage. Too stubborn to declare bankruptcy, Joe tried a number of other businesses with only modest success. Somehow, though, he always managed to pay his bills on time and keep his debts current.

As the years passed, children came along: three sons and one daughter. Margaret saw to it that they were in church every Sunday, but Joe was too busy with work and paying bills. He was happy for them to go, but made it clear to everyone that he considered his own religion a very private matter.

Of their four children, Rachel turned out to have the best business sense of all. By this time the family had opened a diner on Highway 80 just outside Longview. A few years later, Rachel convinced her father to relocate to Interstate 20, which would expose them to all the traffic coming to and from Dallas. It was the biggest gamble of his life, but he went for it, and it soon began to pay off handsomely. Joe, now 62, began to taste the possibility of real success for the first time in his life. Rachel kept the books, did the hiring and firing and proved to be a genius at marketing.

Never before in his life had Joe ever depended on someone else like he did with Rachel. Of course, Margaret had been there to care for the children and keep the house, but this was the first time someone had entered his domain of business. It was uncomfortable at first, but he soon learned to appreciate her innate skills and uncanny instincts.

———————

Joe stood facing the hooded figure for what seemed an eternity. Though human-like in stature, it quickly became apparent that this creature was not from earth. It was dressed in a simple monk's robe which covered its entire body. The face was only partially visible, but Joe could detect what looked like scales on its face, creating a reptilian impression.

Without warning, the creature lightly grasped Joe's hand, and he immediately felt the now familiar sense of acceleration, lifting him above the highest mountain. The hand felt rough and callused, being covered also by a thick, scaly skin.

Silently, they sped through the outer reaches of a kind of desolate no-man's-land. Instead of the shimmering trees and waterfalls, they now seemed to be flying over a swampy area. The sky had turned a dull gray and the air was heavy with mist.

Soon, threatening clouds began to gather low in the distance. Joe expected to see lightning any minute, but instead felt a chill in the air. It seemed dry and cold, like an arctic blast in winter. Continuing on at a rate faster than the speed of sound, the "clouds" became more solid and well defined, becoming a massive wall of mountains rising to a great height directly out of the swamp. Joe also noticed a dot perched on one of the highest peaks. As they raced toward it, the dot became bigger, and soon he could discern the outlines of what appeared to be buildings and towers. With every second that passed, a city began to take shape, until suddenly he found himself, along with his guide, walking down one of its streets.

Joe was about to ask a question, but was immediately stopped by a stern look from his escort.

"Looks like a lizard," he thought as he finally got a good view of the face.

"Sige."* The word came echoing into his mind. "The name of this place is Sige, or, in your language, 'Silence.' For eons, no words, no sounds have been uttered in this land."

"Wadduya know?" thought Joe. "It's like I can hear him in my head, but not with my ears. Maybe I should try."

"Who are you, and what is your name?" thought Joe, directing his attention to his companion.

"I am called Ogdoad."

Just as Joe was about to "think" a follow-up question as to what his name meant, a shadow fell over both of them. They looked up and saw a creature flying through the air.

Years later, he still choked with emotion as he tried to describe his first glimpse of a terar.

"It was so beautiful," he would say, "So overwhelming, that Ogdoad and I and all the others on the street stopped and gasped. Imagine! For the first time in centuries, sounds were heard on the streets of Sige because of the presence of one terar flying overhead. It was like a giant monarch butterfly. The body was about ten feet long and emanated a brilliant light. The wings stretched out at least twenty feet on each side. Yeah, I would say the total wingspan was forty feet. It didn't flit like a butterfly, either. It soared like an eagle, only occasionally moving its powerful wings for forward motion. However, the face was the most impressive of all. It looked somewhat human, yet was as radiant and regal in bearing as a god. Of all the creatures I have seen in heaven, none compared to this."

"Then," he would say with a shadow falling across his face, "I saw myself for the first time. As we watched, trance-like, the terar spread its wings even further, revealing a blinding light that forced my head down. There, in a pool of water, I saw reflected back a hideous creature covered in scars. There were

* pronounced "Sigg-ay"

118

so many scars on my face that I no longer looked human but --
reptilian. Ogdoad! I thought. I looked like Ogdoad!

"I felt a panic welling up inside as I examined the rest of
my body. Until now I hadn't noticed that I, too, was wearing a
monk's robe with a hood. I tore it open and, to my horror, my
whole body was the same. Deep scars so close together and
crisscrossing one another as to give the appearance of scales.

"Ogdoad, apparently oblivious to my shock, 'thought' to
me, 'How fortunate you are to see this terar. They very rarely
are found this far into the frontier. He must be on a mission of
great importance.'

"'Frontier?' I asked. 'What frontier?'

"'Why, the frontier between heaven and hell.'"

"Joe recently became a good friend of mine," began
Pastor Sam Taylor with obvious emotion. "As many of you
know, he was not a church-going man."

A few nervous snickers in the room seemed to confirm
that fact.

Holding up an envelope, Pastor Taylor continued. "I
have in my hand a letter written by Joe after his second heart
attack. He knew that his time was short and dictated this to me
from his hospital bed. He asked me to read it to all of you
today."

Dear Friends and Family,

*If Pastor Sam is reading this letter to you, then it
means I have finally gone for good. Since I've already
had two practice runs, I hope the "real thing" will go
smoothly. I've never been much for words, but I'll do
my best.*

*To Margaret, my sweet wife, I guess you know me
better than anyone. We had a heck of a life, didn't we?*

*I so wanted to do better by you. Please forgive me
for my stubbornness and anger. It wasn't you I was*

119

disappointed in. It wasn't you I was angry at -- it was me. You were the best a man could have.

To my three boys, John, Stephen and Troy. All of you are now men with families of your own. Don't spend your whole life working, like I did. Take more time for your kids; they grow up so fast.

To Rachel, my only daughter. I know you'll do well whatever you decide to do. Don't feel like you must keep the restaurant going for my sake. Sell it if you want and become an architect. (I know that was always your dream.) Just be sure to take care of your mother. That goes for all you kids.

There's one last thing I got to say. It's the main reason I wrote this letter. I asked Pastor Sam to help me with the religious part, but he said it would be better to use my own words, so here goes:

After my second heart attack, Pastor Sam came to see me in the hospital. I had hardly ever been sick a day in my life, and now I was so weak I couldn't even go to the bathroom by myself. Even though I was pretty grouchy and kinda rude to him, deep down it felt good for him to be there.

Pastor Sam said something that made me stop and think. He said, "Joe, I have often thought that two of God's greatest gifts to us are the innocence of childhood and the gradual weakness of old age."

Puzzled, I asked, "What's so great about those?"

"Innocence," he said, "causes children to almost naturally believe in God. They haven't yet experienced the betrayals of teenage and adult life. Then, the weakness of old age has a way of humbling even the proudest and most independent of men."

"You mean men like me."

"Yes, my friend, especially men like you." He took a breath and continued, "Joe, you were robbed of your innocence at the age of ten when your father died. You immediately had to go to work to help support your

family, and you have been doing that your whole life. You always had to be the strong one. Now, it's time for you to be weak. This is a gift from God. He is giving you the chance to let him be strong for you."

Every day I was in the hospital, Pastor Sam stopped by. For the first time in my life I wanted -- no, I had to talk with somebody about God. One day I prayed a prayer, and deep in my heart I knew everything would be okay. I told Pastor Sam I wanted to be baptized as soon as possible. He said, "When you feel stronger, we can do that at church."

"No," I said, "I don't want to wait; can't you do it right here?"

Well, a couple of days later, Pastor Sam sprinkled some water on my head. "In the name of the Father, the Son and the Holy Ghost," he said. Since we were in ICU, only my wife and kids could be there.

Now, I want all of ya'll to know what happened to me, and I want to say this: Don't wait like I did to make peace with God. It's more important than anything else.

"Two weeks later," Pastor Taylor told the congregation, "Joe had a massive heart attack at home and passed away."

Fear, horror, revulsion. These are not emotions one is expected to have in heaven. Now he knew the awful truth. He wasn't in heaven, but some outer "frontier." Maybe he was in, what was that they called it? Purgatory! Maybe he had waited too late for God and missed his chance!

"Ogdoad, where are you taking me?" he demanded.

"To a place in Sige where you will be strengthened for your long journey."

121

"But I've already come so far. I must know the truth. What is my final destination?" Even as he spoke the words, he felt a great weariness descend upon him.

"You modern humans have filled the world with such noise that you've forgotten how to be still. In order to prepare you for heaven, it is vital that your soul learn the healing power of silence."

Puzzled, Joe responded, "I've always been a doer, not a daydreamer. What's the big deal about silence?"

"That's just the problem. You are so busy 'doing' that you have stopped 'being.' Silence is necessary in order to see yourself as you truly are; that's why so many people are afraid of it."

They came to a stop in front of a massive, stone building, and Ogdoad knocked on the ancient, wooden door. A Sigite, a dwarfish, bearded man, answered the door. He led them, without a word, down a long hall to their private chambers. As the door closed behind him, Joe lay down on the bed and fell into an exhausted sleep.

The days spent in Sige proved to be a pleasant interlude from the draining effects of high speed soaring through the atmosphere. The silence was especially refreshing and therapeutic. With each passing day, Joe noticed more spring in his step and a feeling of great energy.

One day, Ogdoad abruptly announced that it was time to leave. Joe wasn't certain how long they'd been there, but had quickly grown accustomed to the invigorating air and long, quiet hikes along mountain paths.

"What kind of creatures are the Sigites?" asked Joe as they resumed their journey, this time on foot. It was the first time he had spoken out loud since their arrival, and the texture of his own voice sounded rich and strong.

Ogdoad appeared puzzled. "They are Sigites; that is all they have ever been. They are as much a part of this mountain as these rocks."

"I mean," asked Joe, "Where did they come from and what is their future, or, do they die like humans?"

122

"No one dies like humans," responded Ogdoad with a shudder. "Of all the worlds in the universe (and there are millions) and of all their inhabitants, none have ever tasted death, save the people of earth. It is the price they must pay for their gift."

"That must be some gift," said Joe, absent-mindedly scratching his head.

"Every race of creatures was given a special gift -- one could even say, a talent. The Sigites, for example, experience wordless, unbroken fellowship with one another. This in turn creates a healing atmosphere for travelers crossing the frontier. Other species and other worlds face their own unique challenges and potentialities. But enough of this. We must ready ourselves for the last stage of our journey."

The whole time they were talking, the two travelers had been walking uphill and now came to a rocky outcropping. As they mounted it, the most fantastic scene imaginable was revealed. Mountain ranges of immense scale stretched out endlessly on every side as far as the eye could see. Clouds drifted below them, revealing intermittent views of what must have been cities seemingly suspended in air without any supports. Yet, slightly above them lay the most spectacular sight of all. A gigantic city built in a perfect cube. It dwarfed all of the mountain peaks and all of the other cities, while it hovered effortlessly above them.

"That," pointed Ogdoad, "is your destination. After your time of cleansing in Sige, you are now summoned to appear before Proarche."

Joe barely heard this bit of news, astonished by what his eyes saw but which his mind could not comprehend. Anthropologists have noted a similar phenomenon when stone age tribesmen encounter the modern world for the first time. In the rain forests of the Amazon or highlands of New Guinea live people whose first sight of a wheel is on the bottom of an airplane! While their eyes can see everything you or I could, their brains cannot process the information. As a result, they do not see an aircraft invented by humans to serve humans; instead, they see a monster. An incomprehensible monster.

As the dumbfounded Joe scanned the horizon, he was visually overwhelmed at the complexity and sophistication of such an abundance of life before him. In the distance he could barely make out small figures flying in and out of the cube-shaped city and asked Ogdoad who these might be.

"Why, terars, of course," came the reply. "Not even the angels are allowed to fly this close to the great city."

"What? No angels in heaven?"

For the first time, Ogdoad chuckled. "Of course there are angels. They are just not permitted to fly here."

"Then how do they get in?"

"You shall see soon enough," spoke Ogdoad as he tightened his belt and pulled his hood close to his face. Then he repeated: "We must prepare ourselves for the last leg of the journey."

Before Joe could speak, the entire vista before them began to shimmer or sparkle, like the trees he had seen at the outset of his journey. The shimmering became more intense, distorting everything around him.

"If I were on earth, I would be sick to my stomach by now," thought Joe.

Instantly, the mountain disappeared and the two travelers found themselves standing in a long corridor. On earth, it would have been a dark tunnel, but here it was lit with a colorful luminescence emanating from the walls, floor and ceiling. They were surrounded with layer upon layer of rubies, sapphires, and emeralds, as well as other precious stones which Joe did not recognize. The effect was somewhat disorienting.

"Where are we?" inquired Joe, turning to Ogdoad.

"We are entering the Great Cube City, the one you just saw from Sige."

"I'll never get used to all these different ways of traveling."

"You shall, soon enough," counseled Ogdoad. "Now we must concentrate on the business at hand."

"Which is what?" questioned Joe, with a note of exasperation in his voice.

Ogdoad stopped and turned to face the Texan. "You are about to meet Proarche. Whatever happens, don't be afraid."

At this point they reached the end of the tunnel, which opened into a great hall of sorts. At one end sat an enormous, empty throne encrusted with the same precious jewels he had just seen. A side door opened and in walked a small figure dressed also in a monk's robe. Actually, the person was slightly taller than Joe, but in that room everything else was dwarfed by the high ceiling and massive throne.

"Proarche," spoke Ogdoad bowing with his face to the floor.

Joe, however, feeling his old, independent nature rising up, remained standing, looking the stranger in the face. And what a face it was! It was even more scarred and scratched than his or Ogdoad's put together.

The two looked at each other for a long moment. Ogdoad tried to pull Joe down to the floor, but he resisted, freeing his arm from the creature's grasp.

Finally, Proarche broke the silence, "You have done well, Ogdoad; please stand." And then to Joe, "We had begun to wonder if you were going to make it here at all."

The sound of Proarche's voice caused Joe to tremble a bit. He was less sure of himself now.

The stranger continued, "Has Ogdoad explained anything to you?"

"No," stammered Joe. "Well, maybe just a little."

"Good. I knew he was the right man for the job."

"Man?" thought Joe, taking a quick glance at his companion.

"People from earth who arrive here fall into two categories: those with strong faith and those with weak faith. The strong are given an angelic escort immediately after death and arrive shortly in my presence. Those who are weaker, like you, need time to adjust. Though you do not recognize it, you are now strong enough to bear the final healing."

125

Joe didn't like the sound of that at all. "Will it hurt?"

"No," replied Proarche, "Not in a physical sense. Your mind, however, could not have endured it, were it not for the preparation in Sige."

He continued, "You must understand that of all the many races and civilizations in the universe, only humans were given the power of choice between good and evil. As a result, your kind fell into an abyss that was almost as deep as hell itself. Your knowledge of evil made you barbaric and cruel. Thus, every time you sinned, a mark was made on your soul, a wound was opened up. In this way it continued, until forgiveness was received. Then, like a physical wound, it was healed, but a scar remained behind for every sin forgiven. Those scars on your body will never go away; they are permanent."

Upon hearing this, Joe bowed his head, pulling his hood over his face and burying his hands in his sleeves. Memories of a life lived without God came flooding back into his mind. Not the "big" sins, but the petty jealousies, angry outbursts, and selfish gloating over the downfall of his competitors. Such great shame! He felt even more repulsive and hopeless. An outcast in heaven itself! Doomed forever to be a hideous creature pitied by all who saw him.

Proarche spoke now with great tenderness. "When the first man and first woman of your race sinned, they were given the gift of shame. It was designed as a protective device or barrier. For most humans, it kept them from descending into ever deeper forms of depravity. I can see that it is still operating effectively in your case. This is the reason why you see your appearance as hideous. It is why you see Ogdoad and myself as members of some alien species."

Joe, by this time, had fallen to his knees, weeping uncontrollably.

Proarche reached forth his hands and spoke the ancient words of healing that had been recited over every human since time began who dared to enter the Great Cubed City. Noah, Abraham, Ruth, Rahab the harlot, St. Peter -- all had wept before Proarche as he touched their heads in the same way he now touched Joe.

Son of Adam, once granted the freedom to sin.
The consequences dire, the cost great.
Now receive the greater freedom -- never to sin again.
Life everlasting, the banishment of shame.

Even as he spoke, the room began to grow bright and the high walls seemed to shrink. In Ogdoad and Joe's places stood two terars in full regalia -- a sight so brilliant that only another terar could have endured it. However, seated on the throne sat a third terar of gigantic proportions. When he spoke, his voice sounded like the crashing of thunderous waves upon the shore.

"Son of Adam no more," he boomed, "Henceforth, you shall be known as 'Bythus.'"

When he conferred upon Joe his new name, the terar stretched out his hands. In both palms were large holes, perfectly round. Shocked, Joe (or Bythus) looked at the bronze feet resting at the bottom of the throne and there also could be seen holes in each one.

"My Lord and my God," was all he could say as he fell to his knees and bowed with his face to the ground.

The terar on the throne stood and reached down to raise the kneeling figure. When standing, his wings folded around his body like a robe, giving him a regal and dramatic appearance.

"Now you understand fully the price I paid. Once a soul has been touched by sin, the scars remain forever -- even if that sin belonged to someone else. Only after your shame was lifted could you have endured this truth. I am Proarche, the firstborn of a new kind, the Alpha and Omega, the prototype, if you will."

"But Sir," responded Joe. "I thought I would bear the scars of sin forever. Now I am transformed into a terar. It doesn't make sense."

"Both are true," replied Proarche. "You are free to assume whichever shape is the most useful for the occasion. The suffering with sin, the receiving of forgiveness, the humbling of ego and the moral victories experienced on earth have all contributed to the type of terar you are now. What you consider your greatest shame -- your scarred soul -- has now become your greatest honor. As a butterfly can only come from a caterpillar, it is the scars themselves that produce the wisest and most magnificent creatures of heaven."

"Now," he continued, "I must introduce you to your traveling companion."

"You mean Og--" He stopped short as he turned and saw, not a lizard, but a terar with a very familiar, human face smiling at him.

"Father?" he said with uncertainty. "But you died when I was ten."

"Yes, and I have waited for you on that snowy mountain ever since. You were never out of my sight for your entire life. I knew you would need help getting here."

The two terars embraced as father and son.

Bythus turned to the throne and asked, "What about my family -- Margaret and my children? Will they make it here also?"

"Yes," came the reply. "We have been expecting Lady Margaret for some time now. Her great faith, which will require merely an angelic escort, is urgently needed elsewhere in the universe. As for your boys, they are blessed with their mother's faith. Rachel, however, like her father, can be very stubborn. I am afraid that she will have a long, yet difficult life."

"But will she make it?"

"Yes, but not without some help."

Joe now knew what he must do.

Sometime later, a reptilian figure in a monk's robe was seen trudging to the top of a snowcapped mountain. He planted himself squarely at the summit, and there he waits to this day.

NOTES

INTRODUCTION
[1]Sir Edward S. Creasy, The Fifteen Decisive Battles of the
  World (New York: The Heritage Press, 1969).
[2]Donald Capps, Deadly Sins and Saving Virtues (Philadelphia:
  Fortress Press, 1987), p. 12.
[3]Thomas Aquinas, Summa Theologica, Trans. by Fathers of the
  English Dominican Province (New York: Benziger Brothers,
  Inc., 1947) Volume I-II, Q.62., Art. 1, p. 851.
[4]2 Corinthians 4:16.
[5]Emil Brunner, Faith, Hope and Love (Philadelphia: The
  Westminster Press, 1956), p. 13.
[6]Matthew 16:25. Augustine, as always, states this paradox
  succinctly and brilliantly. "If you love your soul, there is
  danger that it may perish. Therefore, you are not permitted to
  love it, since you do not want it to perish. But in not wanting
  it to perish, you love it." [cited in Josef Pieper, Faith, Hope,
  Love (San Francisco: Ignatius Press, 1986), p. 243.]

A WOMAN CALLED MARA
[1]Adapted from Ruth, Chapter 1.

PART ONE: ANGER
[1]Michael Camile, Gothic Art Glorious Visions (New York:
  Harry N. Abrams, Inc., 1996), p. 38.
[2]Ruth 1:20-21
[3]Ruth 4:14-15.
[4]Carol Tavris, Anger: The Misunderstood Emotion (New York:
  Simon and Schuster, 1982), p. 300.
[5]*Ibid.*, p. 300.

A WITCH AND A KING
[1]Adapted from I Samuel, Chapter 28.

PART TWO: ENVY
[1]Edgar A. Poe, Selected Stories and Poems Edgar Allan Poe (New York: Airmont Books, 1962), p. 170.
[2]I Samuel 18:7.
[3]Robert S. McGee, The Search For Significance (Houston, TX: Rapha Publishing, 1990), pp. 63-65.
[4]Henry David Thoreau, Walden and "Civil Disobedience" (New York: Airmont Publishing Co., Inc., 1965), p. 229.
[5]Soren Kierkegaard, Purity of Heart Is To Will One Thing Trans. by Douglas V. Steere (New York: Harper & Brothers Publishers, 1948), pp. 180-181.

THE PROPHET BIGOT
[1]Adapted from Jonah, Chapter 1.

PART THREE: PRIDE
[1]Donald Capps, Deadly Sins And Saving Virtues (Philadelphia: Fortress Press, 1987), p. 98.
[2]Marvin Olasky, The Tragedy of American Compassion (Washington D.C: Regney Publishing, Inc., 1992), p. 99.
[3]This is not to deny the progress that has been made in American race relations. Things have improved dramatically over the past thirty or so years. However, we still have a long way to go.
[4]Michael P. Green, Editor, Illustrations for Biblical Preaching (Grand Rapids, MI: Baker Book House, 1982), p. 198.
[5]Psalms 102:25-27.
[6]Galatians 6:10.

THE DISILLUSIONED KING
[1]Story inspired by the book of Ecclesiastes.

PART FOUR: SLOTH
[1]Evagrius Ponticus, cited in Siegfried Wenzel, The Sin of Sloth: Acedia (Chapel Hill, N. Carolina: The University of North Carolina Press, 1967), p. 5.

PART FOUR: SLOTH, continued

[2]Dorothy Sayers, cited in Henry Fairlie, <u>The Seven Deadly Sins Today</u> (Notre Dame, Indiana: University of Notre Dame Press, 1979), p. 114.

[3]Ecclesiastes 1:1.

[4]Ecclesiastes 2:17-20.

[5]Orrin E. Klapp, <u>Overload and Boredom: Essays on the Quality of Life in the Information Society</u> (New York: Greenwood Press, 1986), p. 23.

[6]Hyrum W. Smith, <u>The 10 Natural Laws of Successful Time and Life Management</u> (New York: Warner Books Inc., 1994), p. 25.

[7]Proverbs 6:6-8.

[8]Thoreau, *op. cit.,* p. 14.

[9]Aquinas, *op. cit.,* I.II.40, p. 6.

[10]Josef Pieper <u>Faith, Hope, Love</u> (Ignatius Press: San Francisco, 1986), p. 110.

[11]*Ibid.,* p. 111.

[12]Psalm 42:11.

HE DIED A SLAVE

[1]Adapted from Numbers, Chapter 11.

PART FIVE: GLUTTONY

[1]C.S. Lewis, <u>The Abolition of Man</u> (New York: Macmillan Publishing Co., 1955), p. 35.

[2]Gerald G. May, <u>Addiction & Grace</u> (San Francisco: Harper Collins Publishers, 1991), pp. 54-55.

[3]Isaiah 42:3a.

THE MISER BECOMES A TRAITOR

[1]Adapted from John, Chapter 12.

PART SIX: GREED

[1]Matthew 6:26-30.

[2]Michael P. Green, <u>Illustrations for Biblical Preaching</u>, *op. cit.,* p. 393.

PART SIX: GREED, continued
[3]Luke 15:11-32.
[4] Luke 12:16-21.
[5]John Stossel, June 16,1997, http://www.204.202.137.116/onair
   /abcnewsspecials/transcripts/stossel990311_trans.html
[6]Colossians 3:23-24.
[7]I John 4:19.
[8]Matthew 6:24.

HOW THE MIGHTY HAVE FALLEN
[1]Adapted from Judges, Chapter 16.

PART SEVEN: LUST
[1]Philip Yancey, *Christianity Today*, "The Lost Sex Study,"
   December 12, 1994, p. 80.
[2]*Ibid.*, p. 80.
[3]Laurie Hall, An Affair of the Mind (Focus on the Family:
   Colorado Springs, CO, 1996), p. 76.
[4]I Corinthians 13:7.
[5]Judges 16:15-16.
[6]I Corinthians 13:13.

Order today the **Teacher's Manual** for *Getting to the Root.*

Pastors, Sunday School teachers and Home Group leaders have all discovered a great resource in this fourteen lesson guide to the seven deadly sins. Each sin is divided into two lessons: the first delves into the problem of anger, envy, pride, etc., while the second focuses upon the solutions.

Each lesson has at least four discussion questions, a helpful outline, examples and practical applications to everyday life. We also provide a master student handout for each lesson that the teacher can duplicate. (Altogether, 64 pages of notes and 22 pages of reproducible handouts.)

PRICING INFORMATION

Getting to the Root book   - $11.95 + $3.00 shipping

    Volume discounts are available:

      5 - 9 books $9.00 + shipping

      10 or more $8.00 + shipping

Teacher's Manual $25.00 + $3.00 shipping

    (Comes in a sturdy 3 ring binder.)

ORDERING INFORMATION

Write to: Legacy Press
P.O. Box 773096
Houston, TX 77215-3096
Call Toll Free: 1-888-323-1868
Web Site: www.gettingtotheroot.com
Email: gettingtotheroot@aol.com